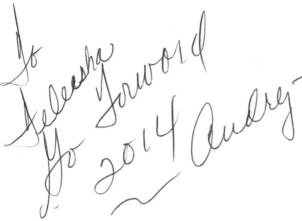

To Seleasha
Go Forword
2014 Audrey

On the Way Here: The Path That Chose Me

Audrey Lee Watkins

PublishAmerica
Baltimore

© 2009 by Audrey Lee Watkins.
All rights reserved. No part of this book may be reproduced, stored in a retrieval system or transmitted in any form or by any means without the prior written permission of the publishers, except by a reviewer who may quote brief passages in a review to be printed in a newspaper, magazine or journal.

First printing

All characters in this book are fictitious, and any resemblance to real persons, living or dead, is coincidental.

PublishAmerica has allowed this work to remain exactly as the author intended, verbatim, without editorial input.

ISBN: 1-60703-241-4
PUBLISHED BY PUBLISHAMERICA, LLLP
www.publishamerica.com
Baltimore

Printed in the United States of America

All scripture quoted from the King James Version.

On the Way Here

Standing here in this place I begin to ask,
Why getting here has been such a task
Many strange trials began to appear,
I stumbled and fell a few times
On the Way Here

This place of peace has me free from doubt,
Situations like mazes yet I know I'll come out
Confusion on this path led to many a tear,
For the friends and family I lost
On The Way Here

I believed in God and He established me,
Believing His prophet brought prosperity
With this new confidence there's nothing to fear,
Even on the mountains that I had to climb
On The Way Here

My blessed Savior found without sin,
You gave your life so that I may live again
Thank you my shepherd and overseer,
For redeeming a wretch like me
On The Way Here

Here in this place is the peace of God,
That peace that He promised would guard my heart
Now I didn't say that I had arrived,
I'm just simply saying that I have survived
Through the muck and mire God's made crystal clear,
The Lord opened up my eyes
On The Way Here

Audrey Watkins
Copyright 2006

Acknowledgments

I would like to take this opportunity to acknowledge my parents, Odie Wells and J.D Moore without whom this journey could never have taken place. Thank you for everything that you taught me. To my Grandmother, Inez, I love you. I thank and praise God for all of my siblings, too many to name but you know who you are.

I want to thank God for blessing me with my children, Nicole', Charles, Hope, Ciara, and Tyree. Without the initial desire to make things better for them, I am not certain where I would be today. Thank you Nicole' for being there for me, and much love to you and Charles for learning to forgive me. I love you all.

To my spiritual family, Drs. Milton & Brenda Woods, thank you for teaching me how to live victoriously, and thank you for being such great examples. Thank you Bethel family.

To the women who taught me to fight my addiction naturally, Eileen Poole, Claudinia Buford, and Sara Ruebin, God Bless You and Thank You!

Introduction

Childhood sexual abuse reached epidemic proportions between 1980 and 1990 with a 322 percent increase. It's estimated that 60 million survivors live in America today. Long-term effects of childhood sexual abuse include; fear, anxiety, depression, anger, hostility, inappropriate sexual behavior, poor self-esteem, tendency toward substance abuse, and difficulty with close relationships.

This is a textbook example of how these behaviors played out in the life of this woman. Leah's life is on an out of control spiral as she struggles to find relief from the pain and loneliness. Against all odds she continues her journey, "On The Way Here"

A few years ago, a young lady with five children walked into church and accepted Jesus Christ into her life. No one could imagine at that time what she laid at His feet—all the years of abuse, mental suffering, bondage, addictions, habits and a hunger and desire to be free. The young lady who walked into the church is the author of this book. Audrey is free today by the grace and power of God.

I am proud to serve as her Bishop, her spiritual leader and guide. I as well as the membership of the church have watched Audrey grow, flourish and prosper as a newly created vessel (or woman) of God.

Within the pages of this book, you will experience a journey from losing battles to victory, from bondages to freedoms, from claiming to be a victim to knowing she is the victor. There will be times when reading this book you will see yourself and put the book down because you can't read on. Read on—this book lets you know you can make it. Allow this book to be a testimony to you that your struggles may be different but you can achieve the same result.

What you may consider impossible, is possible—you've just have to be willing to let go of the past and move forward in your life. You must have a vision of who you are and who you want to be. You were not created for failure. You are not defeated. Allow *On the Way to Here* to be a turning point in your life. Don't let your reading be in vain.

This book is a must read, life-changing, riveting account of what God can do in an individuals life when they yield their life to God. I call it a true 'rags to riches' story.

Dr. Milton C. Woods

CHAPTER ONE
The Beginning

How do you begin to unburden your soul of the issues that kept you bound for so long? This story is the personal recollection of a woman, who like many women, found herself on a journey that she believed would never end. This journey would span over three decades and would take her places she never wanted to go, and keep her there much, much longer than she wanted to stay.

It was just about nightfall on the north end of Detroit. Six-year-old Leah hated the nightfall, there always seemed to be something evil lurking in it, especially on the weekend. Saturday night on the north end of Detroit was alive and popping for all the major players of that time. Pimps, prostitutes, dance halls, pool halls and after hours joints made up the neighborhood atmosphere. Tires screeching, music playing, people yelling and arguing in a drunken slur, and Momma and Daddy not at home again. At least there was some solace in that fact or was there? Momma and Daddy not being at home meant that at least she didn't have to hear them argue or see them fight, at least not for a few more hours

What should have been a haven for young Leah would turn out to be, the place where nightmares began. A seven-room walk up on the corner of Brush and Kenilworth. The building took up the entire corner and not only housed the walk-up but also two stores. The one directly on the corner was affectionately known as "the confectionery," which was a small grocery store and the other one was called "Dempsy's" a local family owned beer and wine store. The rest of the building, which took up a half of block, was an empty storefront, the walk-up separated the grocery store and Dempsy's. All of the players in the neighborhood lurked around these corners. Always making some kind of evil deal and watching the neighborhood girls.

But there was another evil lurking in the dark of their upstairs flat. One so horrible that the instant that she thought about it, it was as if a bolt of lightening had struck in her very soul shocking her out of the deep thought that she had found herself in. She was frightened as she looked around the flat, yet all of the other eight children seemed unaffected by her thoughts and fears.

As she looked around she saw her oldest sister Anna, and immediately, her fears subsided. As long as Anna was around she didn't have to worry about the cruel, cruel monster that lurked in the dark. She scooted over to the couch and sat next to her sister to watch The Green Hornet. "Step on it Kato" she heard her and her sister say in unison, and they both began to laugh. For a few brief moments she felt like a normal six-year-old. She paid no attention as the phone rang and her sister got up from the couch to answer it.

By now some of her other sisters and one of her brothers had joined her in the living room and they were all excitedly watching The Green Hornet so she did not hear Anna tell her boyfriend to come on over to pick her up. She continued to laugh, play, and watch television until she heard the sound of a car radio down on the street. It got her attention, she hoped that it was her parents returning early for one of those rare nights when they would drink at home and then lock themselves in the bedroom, but she was not that lucky.

She heard a car horn, then someone running down the stairs so she jumped up, ran to the window and stuck her head out just in time to see Anna opening the passenger door of a powder blue convertible. "Anna," she cried, "Don't leave me." But her sister was excited to go out with her boyfriend in his new car. They made a beautiful couple, she had on a bright red lace party dress and he was dressed in all white. "Get back in the window" she screamed at her, "Now!" "No, I don't want you to go" Leah cried louder. "Get back in that window before I tell Momma on you," Anna said.

Somehow the fear of Momma over rode the fear of the monster momentarily, and she put her head back in the window but continued to watch as the powder blue convertible drove away and disappeared around the corner. If Anna knew what kind of monster she was leaving her with she would not have left her. But she didn't know, or at least Leah hadn't told her. Why don't little girls tell? She was afraid, afraid of the monster, afraid of her mother, afraid that everyone would think that it was her fault because that's what the monster said.

"Nobody is going to believe you and even if they do they don't care, if they did they wouldn't leave you here with me all the time" the monster would tell her. To a six-year-old this made a lot of sense so she kept quiet. Now that Anna was gone a new unfamiliar kind of fear gripped Leah. A fear that she had never experienced before and now what a few minutes ago felt like the worst kind of fear became the only security that was available to her. She swallowed hard as she heard the monster say from the back of the flat, "Get out of that window and come back here with me."

So she made her way back to the room in the back of the flat and sat on the bed waiting for the monster to do what monsters do to little girls. She lay there numb trying her best to block out the physical pain. She wanted it to be over so that at least she could fall asleep in his bed and be safe from whatever or who ever else might be laying in wait for her. Soon it was over but as she began to drift off voices in the distance told her that her parents were home. As usual on a Saturday night she could tell that they had been drinking and fighting. She didn't want to hear them argue or see them fight, but most of all she didn't want them to know that she was in the monster's room. She was afraid that somehow they might be able to tell. "Brother!" She heard her Momma call from the stairs, "Come and help me." "Now what," she heard the monster say and she covered her head and pretended to be asleep as he got up to see what was going on.

In the distance Leah could hear a lot of commotion in the bathroom. Leah pulled the pillow more tightly over her head. Eventually, she fell asleep but only for a short period of time. When she started to stir she realized that the monster had not come back to bed. She became frightened but somehow managed to gather up enough courage to find out what was going on. She slid from the bed careful not to make a sound; she went to the bedroom door and peeked down the long hallway. There was no one there so she ventured into the hallway carefully creeping so as not to wake anyone. The first door that she came to was the bathroom.

The door was slightly opened, so she pushed it all the way. There was blood everywhere. She was paralyzed with fear but somehow managed to step all the way into the bathroom. There were bloody handprints on the wall, on the towels, and all over the bathtub. The blood on the tub got her attention so she moved closer. "Oh My God," she heard herself say. There in the tub were the clothes that her father was wearing when he left home, yesterday. What could have happened to him? Leah began to cry. "Where is my Daddy?"

She ran to the front of the flat where her parent's room was, but the door was wide open and they were gone. Just as she was about to let out a loud scream she heard someone stir on the couch. " What are you doing up this time of night?" It was Anna back from her date. The fear that she felt instantly melted and she once again felt safe. "I was looking for Momma and Daddy" Leah said. "I heard them come in earlier." "Yeah, they left back out" Anna said sleepily. "Anna there is blood all over the bathroom and all over Daddy's clothes" Leah told her. "Yeah" said Anna, "they been fighting again but he's o.k, get up here and go to sleep"

Once again Leah felt safe, Anna was home. Leah wanted so badly to talk to her about the monster, but just like her parents, he was gone, at least for the night. She snuggled up next to her sister and again for a brief period in time she felt like a normal little girl. She felt secure and she began to imagine that Anna was really Batgirl and was able to protect her from anything and anybody. Her hero was home and she didn't have to worry about any more monsters or blood or fights, at least not for the rest of the night. "Move over" Anna said and snapped her out of her daydream. But it was o.k. because she knew she wasn't going to move far. She also knew that Anna would be there when she woke up in a few hours. There were few things that she could take comfort in, the love that she and her sister shared was at the very top of that short list.

Morning came and when Leah woke up and looked at her parent's bedroom door it was closed. Anna was already up and moving around, cooking and cleaning. Before a smile could form on Leah's face the bedroom door opened and her Daddy came out of the room. She ran to give him a hug but when she touched him he groaned with pain. Daddy wasn't o.k. Momma had hurt him bad. She had used a broken beer bottle and cut him on the neck. He was fighting back the tears when he told her that he had to leave.

Daddy left and Leah realized that this fight was different from all of the others. She wanted to go and peek into the room and make sure that her Momma was o.k. but she was afraid. She looked up at Anna and could tell that she had been crying. She didn't understand, Anna never cried, or at least she never saw her. "What's wrong Anna?" she asked, but Anna said, "nothing go get some clothes on." She went, but for the first time she knew that Anna wasn't telling the truth.

Things were very different after that, a few days later Grandma came over. She, Momma, Daddy, and Anna were in Momma and Daddy's bedroom talking. Anna came out crying and ran to the back of the flat. She wouldn't tell Leah what was wrong but it must have been something really bad. Grandma came out a little later and had also been crying. She greeted and hugged all of them and left. It wasn't long after Grandma left that the big fight started.

The door was closed but you could hear them cussing and fighting. Leah ran to the door to listen. All the kids were crying now and Anna just began to scream. Leah heard glass breaking and then what sounded like the window opening. She heard her Daddy scream as if he was falling from the top of the world and that's when she heard the gunshots. She wasn't sure how many, pop, pop, pop, she heard. She was terrified, just then Brother came and burst open the bedroom door. He ran over to the window and pulled Momma in. She was leaning out of the window and shooting up in the air. Leah ran to another window to look out for her Daddy. She could barely make him out, running, limping down the street but he was alive. "Run Daddy, run" she cried.

"If I was really trying to kill him he would be dead," Momma said, "I was just trying to scare him, teach him a lesson." All the kids gathered around her except for Anna and Leah. Leah wasn't sure why Anna was so afraid, but she was certain now that if Momma were to find out about her and the monster she would probably kill them both. She made up her mind right then and there that she would never know, she would never tell.

Note to all monsters; 2nd Chronicles 7:10 "If my people, which are called by my name, shall humble themselves and pray, seek my face and turn from their wicked ways, then I will hear from the heavens and will forgive their sins and I will heal their land"

Monsters need forgiveness too. To all of the monsters in my life, those who knew that they were monsters and the ones that had no idea, I forgive you. Take this time to seek God and to ask him to forgive you and become your personal savior as He has become mine. You too can be made whole.

CHAPTER TWO

They couldn't stay in the flat after that. Leah really wasn't sure why but they had to move. Daddy was gone and Leah was afraid for him to come back. They moved into a big house in a different neighborhood. Again Momma was gone most of the time and she saw very little of her father for what seemed like an eternity. The house that they moved into was physically a better place but the mentality was the same. The monster still lurked in the dark but with Daddy only around part of the time the monster stepped up his game and included Leah's other sisters in his demonic scheme.

None of them told, fear of Momma and what the monster would do to them if they told kept them all quiet. His being there was one of the reasons that Momma was able to go out and party with her friends. She wouldn't stand for anyone messing that up. Anna was busy with her new boyfriend these days so Leah had learned to stay under the radar and take care of herself. It seemed that everywhere she looked some one was either having sex or talking about it. You would think that it didn't help that the new house was right next door to the neighborhood after hours joint, but in a lot of ways this was a blessing.

The woman that ran the after hours joint was called Big Momma. She was a stern woman but she had a heart of gold. She welcomed the neighborhood kids in to laugh at the drunks while having a snack in her humongous kitchen. She also allowed the girls from next door to come in and dance for the guys. She would kill them dead if they even thought about touching one of them and she always made sure they had something to eat and a few cents in their pocket for the ice-cream truck or candy from the "Penny Store."

Big Momma had a grown daughter, named Vette. Vette had three young sons that she had adopted, Al, Bobby, and Mickey. They were about the same ages as Leah and her two older sisters, Lynn and Ina. The six of them became inseparable, always outside playing hide-and-go-seek, or Chase, Red

Light-Green Light or Simon Says. When they weren't outside playing they were inside Big Momma's house laughing, eating, and dancing.

Big Momma spent a lot of time with the neighborhood kids. They all loved and respected her. That year (1967), she would gather all of the families together and head them up to Belle Isle for a Fourth of July picnic. There the kids would enjoy canoeing, horseback riding, baseball, volleyball and all the food you could ever think of eating. It was one of the few good times that Leah would be able to remember. Too bad the good times wouldn't last very long.

There was a spirit of unrest in the city of Detroit back then. The "Big Four," a squad of policemen known mostly for their meanness, roamed the streets harassing the black citizens of Detroit with little if any consequences. They stopped young blacks, asking degrading questions, roughing them up if they didn't give the answers they wanted to hear. This was a common and accepted practice back then. Even the few black policemen joined in on the Gestapo tactics and the people of Detroit were growing tired of it.

A week after the picnic Leah heard Daddy's voice early in the morning. Daddy had been around a lot more lately, and she was happy about that. Momma and Daddy weren't nearly as mean to each other as they had been in the past. She lay there smiling thinking that for the first time in a long time, she had heard her Daddy singing an old blues song, as he was getting ready to go to work a few mornings earlier. *'I'll drink when I wanta, and play a little poker too, dontcha say nothing to me, as long as I'm takin care of you, as long as I'm working baby, and payin all the bills, I don't want no mouth from you, I found the way I'm supposed to liiive, you must be crazy woman, oh you just gotta be out of yo mind, as long as I'm footin the bills woman, I'm payin the coost to be the boss.'* It was in that moment that Leah realized that Daddy was back home and that made her really happy.

But what was he doing home this time of morning? He should have left for work hours ago. Maybe it was earlier than she thought; the sun was shining bright on a hot summer morning in early July. She sat up in the bed trying to figure out what time it was. Just then she heard a blood-curdling scream coming from her Momma downstairs. She and her sisters and brother jumped out of her bed and ran downstairs to see what was going on. What they saw would cause Leah to have nightmares for a very long time.

Brother was getting out of a police car, he had bandages everywhere, and he was bloody and beaten. They had beaten him in the face so badly that now he really looked like a monster. His eyes were swollen shut and he had stitches in his head, which was at least twice the size of any ones she had ever saw. The police were trying to talk to Momma and tell her what had happened but she was screaming and crying and didn't hear a word they were saying. They told Daddy that Brother was with another man who was wanted by the police and that they had resisted arrest. The other man was dead and Brother was very lucky.

Momma took Brother into the house and began to ask him questions about what had happened. He could barely talk but he attempted to tell her. Of course his story was completely different than that of the police but there was nothing that could be done about it. So many people were complaining about how the police were treating them back then but no one was listening. Dr. King was on the news almost every day telling the people not to fight back but they were tired of hearing that. They were ready to take matters into their own hands.

After things calmed down in the house Leah began to think about what she had just saw. The police had really beaten Brother up badly but she was having a hard time being sad for him. Her feelings kept shifting from sadness to satisfaction to sadness but the sadness was not for Brother, it was for her Momma who was so upset. The satisfaction was in thinking that somehow God had punished Brother for what he had been doing to her and her sisters.

All the talk around the neighborhood was that one way or another the police were going to pay for what they did to Brother. Momma wanted to sue and did contact a lawyer, but the men in the neighborhood got drunker and angrier and were planning some type of physical retaliation. They would not have to wait long to get their revenge.

On July 23rd 1967 the "Big Four" raided an after hours joint on the west side of Detroit. They beat up and arrested over 50 people and that was about as much as the black city of Detroit residents could take. The infamous 1967 riots began on that day. Leah remembered Daddy coming home early from work and saying something like, "Ain't no fun when the rabbit got the gun," and he and Brother took off down the street. A few minutes later they came running back into the house with their arms full of beer and wine. Daddy tripped and fell on the way in and silver dollars splattered all over the living room floor. They laughed and celebrated their own stupidity and left right back out of the house.

For the next few days the city burned. Leah remembered Momma was so worried and tired. Worried because Daddy and Brother were out robbing and looting with the rest of the thugs in the city, and tired because for hours at a time she stood outside with the water hose, watering down the roof so that their house would not catch on fire.

The flames seemed to rain from the sky during the day. At night the sky was lit up for as far as the eyes could see. Daddy and Brother would come and bring looted merchandise to the house and then leave again. Momma would watch the news and on several occasions saw Daddy's car. Leah heard a reporter ask if anyone had any information on the owner of the car to contact the police. Everything was so crazy and all Leah could do at this point was stay close to Momma and do whatever she asked.

One good thing had come out of all the new turmoil in Leah's life. Brother's attention was somewhere else. By the time she would see him he would either be too tired or too drunk to bother with her. Not to mention that Leah had found a new place by Momma's side these days. Leah had a lot of new fears such as if the policemen were going to catch Daddy and Brother and finish what they started with Brother and kill her Daddy. This fear would be short lived because when the National Guard were called into the city it made it a little harder for them to get out and loot. Finally after five days the chaos was over but a new form of chaos began. So much had changed in those five days, so much destruction, she just did not understand.

Not all of the changes were bad. Leah's family had new clothes, furniture, and so much food that she had to help Momma bury some in the backyard. They had looted grocery stores, furniture stores, clothing stores, and jewelry stores. They had so much new stuff that didn't know what to do with most of it. Some of the families on their block had taken their old stuff and set it out for the garbage man. But when the police saw their old things setting out they waited until the garbage men picked up the things and then went into the people's homes and confiscated the new things. Momma said that would happen so she moved all of the old things into the basement just in case and started looking for a new place to live.

They didn't find a new place right away. The neighborhood was devastated. Everywhere you looked you would see where businesses used to be. Empty shells of buildings that left the city horribly maimed. In the midst of all the ashes and destruction a routine was formed. Every Sunday morning

Leah and her sisters, Lynn, Ina, Jean, Denise, and Renee along with Big Momma's Grand boys would go to a small Baptist church not far from where they lived. Morning View Baptist Church. After church they had a variety of places they would go.

If they decided to go skating, the older girls would go with the Big Momma's grand boys to a place called the Arcadia. Leah wasn't a very good skater so she and her two younger sisters would go home and help Momma cook. Nor did Leah like to fight which is what usually happened when they went skating so she was happy to go home with Momma. If they decided to go to the movies, then they all could go so she spent lots of Sunday afternoons watching Clint Eastwood movies.

There was another place that they went on occasion. Leah had two Uncles who knew lots of people in the music industry. Uncle Man was a partner in a club called the Soul Expression. The club sponsored a new T.V. dance show called The Soul Train. It was a very popular spot for the young adult crowd through the week but on Sunday afternoon Uncle Man and his partner would open up the club to the local teenagers. It made Leah and her sisters very popular to have this kind of connection. This was an awesome time in Leah's life. She began to look forward to Sundays starting with church, and it didn't matter where Sunday ended because for the first time in her young life all of the options were good, as long as they started with church on Sunday morning.

The next few months flew past. There was still unrest in the neighborhood. Now Momma had to go a long way to get to a super market because they had burned down all of the stores in the neighborhood during the riot. Anna had gotten engaged and was expecting her first baby. Momma still wanted to move but had not yet found the right place. Daddy was around less and less again. All of these changes didn't really frighten Leah; she had long since learned not to be so afraid. God had brought her and her family through all of the bad stuff and they were still alive and kicking.

The climate of the times was still chaotic. Leah and her sisters and young brother were all in a new school. Leah had begun to understand that she was a little brighter than most of he kids in her class. She began to enjoy school and looked forward to it as much as she looked forward to going to church. It was on one of those school days when tragedy would strike again.

CHAPTER THREE

It was a cold gray day in March and school was dismissed early. She walked the twelve blocks home with her sisters. All around her kids were crying and everyone was trying to hurry and get home before something ugly started up again. Leah came home to find Momma glued to the television. They had made the announcement at school. Someone had shot Dr. King and they wanted us to hurry and get home for fear that there would be another riot. Momma was very scared and was more determined than ever to get her kids out of that neighborhood.

Most of the time we were there alone. Daddy had started to stay out more and more and Momma felt that the only way to protect her children was to get them out of that neighborhood. Leah didn't want to move again. She loved her school and her church and she knew those things would have to change. She had no idea just how much things would change.

Momma got Pa-Pa to co-sign for the new house. The house was on the outskirts of Detroit in a much better community. It seemed from the very beginning that this place would be a haven for Leah. Little did she know that this would be the place where years of abuse would start all over again.

This new place started out to be perfect. It was a big beautiful four-story home. In the basement there were eight rooms. They could play hide-and-go-seek all day long. On the first floor there was the living room, den, dining room, kitchen, and bathroom. On the second floor there were three bedrooms and a bathroom, and on the third floor there was another three bedrooms and a bathroom. Out side the window of Lynn and Ina's room there was a fire escape that led from the third floor to the ground.

Leah's new school was just down the street. Now instead of walking to church on Sunday, Pa-Pa would come and pick them up and drive them to a brand new church in a brand new building. There was always family and friends around partying, dancing and laughing. It seemed that their new house was the place to be, that was until all the trouble started. To make things even better Daddy's job was right in the neighborhood. What wasn't so good was the fact that so was one of Daddy's new girlfriends.

The first sign of trouble began when her Daddy not only decided to leave, but he would move in with another woman. Momma was mad all of the time. She talked bout going to the woman's house and breaking windows, setting fires and a lot of other bad things. But to Leah's knowledge she never did any of these things. She would though, get together with her friends and bash him for hours at a time while they drank. Leah and her sisters hated when she did this and one night they decided to take action.

They took some of Momma's trash bags and packed some of their clothes in them. Lynn and Ina's room was on the third floor; it was the room where you could access the fire escape. They had decided that they would not listen to one more bad word about their Daddy. They took their bags of clothes and down the fire escape they went. When they got to the bottom of the fire escape, they took off down the alley vowing never to return home again. The new house was located five houses from the corner. They had been gone all of three minutes when they got to the end of the alley. As soon as they peeked their heads around the corner there was their Daddy driving down the street.

They all could have won marathons that night. They ran back to the house, up the fire escape, back into the window and jumped into the bed, clothes and all. Just about then they heard Daddy come in downstairs. Momma immediately tore into him but he didn't want to hear what she was saying. "Where are the girls?" Leah heard him ask. "Upstairs in the bed, where do you think they are this time of night?" Momma answered sarcastically. "I think that I just saw them running down the alley," their Daddy answered her question. "Man you are crazy," Momma screamed.

In the meantime the girls took that opportunity to get out of their clothes and pretend to be asleep. Their Daddy made his way up the stairs, but by the time he made it all the way up to the third floor, the girls were out of their clothes and into their innocence roles. Daddy didn't even mention to them at that time that he thought that he had seen them outside, they all appeared so angelic. One thing that they didn't have to pretend, they were genuinely happy to see him. Leah took this opportunity to ask the forbidden question, "Daddy when are you coming back home?" Daddy said what he always said and that was that he didn't know when he would be home. He didn't say he wasn't though and that gave Leah and her sisters hope that someday he would. Too bad someday never came.

Pa-Pa came around though; he would buy them special treats and take them to special places. Anna had her own key to Pa Pa's apartment. She would go there and clean and he would give her money. Leah absolutely loved going to church with Pa-Pa. He would cook great dinners and tell funny stories about the old south and the revenuers chasing him. Leah would help him cook and clean up afterwards.

Anna got married in a beautiful ceremony. Her husband had joined the Air Force and had gone to prepare a place for Anna and her two children. She was as happy as she could be and looking forward to joining her husband soon. She had no idea that she would literally have to fight for her life before she left to join her husband.

Leah was actually enjoying being a kid for a change. The elementary school was directly across the street and it had a playground with swings and games during the summer months. Everyday they would put out all of the equipment for t-ball, arts and crafts, softball, horseshoes, as well as board games. Her favorite game was battleship and she was very good at it. She would play for hours at a time beating all of the kids and most of the adults who dared to take her on. She was also the family first baseman in all of their softball games and enjoyed playing that position as well.

It was a beautiful summer day. All of the kids were outside playing. The neighborhood was full of families with lots of children. On the street where Leah lived there were two extremely large families. Leah's family was one of them. There were seven girls and two boys in her immediate family, but there were always cousins and in-laws around as well as lots of friends.

The other family was even larger than Leah's. This family, the Jacksons' had more children than Leah's family. They were all very tall and healthy. They had recently moved to Michigan from Mississippi as a lot of people did back then. The Jacksons' in a lot of ways were larger than life. Leah's sister Denise often played with the younger sister Debbie. Debbie and Denise were basically the same age and for the most part played well together. One day as most children will Debbie and Denise got into a fight. Now Debbie had not yet begun to grow as tall as the rest of her family so she and Denise were pretty much the same size. On this particular day it was Denise that got the better of the two.

It goes without saying that Debbie ran home to tell her mom that she had just gotten beat up. Her sister Mammie was not to pleased to hear that her little sister had gotten beat up and she decided to take matters into her own hands. That was a big mistake. At the school across the street there was a big lot on the corner, it was the grass lot where children weren't supposed to play but they did. That is where Debbie and Denise got into their fight and because she felt she had not done anything except defend herself that is where Denise stayed while Debbie ran home to tell her family about the fight.

Denise was a fighter so it didn't frighten her when she saw Debbie and Mammie coming down the street; in fact she stood up and squared off with them as Mammie began to question her about the fight. When she admitted fighting Debbie, Mammie, who was seventeen years old and six feet two inches tall hauled off and hit Denise who was less than five feet and only ten years old. Denise, being who she is never backed down, she hit Mammie back and they began to fight. Denise never backed down and her baby sister Renee knew that she wouldn't. She also knew that they needed help so she ran the couple of houses down to tell her family what was going on.

Leah and the rest of her family members were inside the house. Most of the people who were there including cousins and friends were just sort of hanging out. One cousin was up under the kitchen sink trying to replace a busted pipe and Leah was watching him. She loved watching him because she thought that he was so handsome and smart. That's when ten-year-old Renee burst into the house. "Mammie is beating up Denise!" she cried. At that point all hell broke loose in the house. Leah's cousin nearly knocked his own head off trying to get from up under the sink. When he did get up he brought the pipe wrench with him. Out the door he ran along with all the other sisters, brothers, uncles, cousins and friends who had armed themselves with all sorts of household items. Momma had taught them that there was no such thing as a fair fight. She said always bring an equalizer to the battle in case the other person started to get the best of you.

Leah's two inseparable sisters Lynn and Ina got to the grass lot first. Mammie was bent over Denise trying to hit her but Denise was a scraper, she was kicking and moving making it impossible for Mammie to hit her. Ina ran up behind her and hit her in the back of the head and when she stood up and turned to hit Ina, Lynn jumped her from behind. They beat her up bad but

Mammie was a fighter also and she wasn't going down without a fight. When she made her final attempt to fight back, out came the knife. One of the girls stabbed Mammie in the arm.

In the meantime Debbie had run back to her house and gotten her family. The two families descended on the grass lot and it was the Hatfield's and the McCoy's revisited. Half of the family was fighting and the other half was trying to stop the rest of them from fighting. Leah ran to her sister Denise to make sure that she was o.k. Mammie had gotten in a few good licks on her but Denise had held her own. Leah held on to her just the same. It seemed for a brief moment that the ones that were trying to break up the fight were going to be successful until the Jackson's Mom hit Momma.

Now, the ones who were trying to stop the fight joined in the fight and the neighborhood watched as the Jacksons and the Morrises tried to kill each other. Since the Morrises has been in the neighborhood longer and had a reputation already for fighting most of the neighbors that openly took sides took the Morrises side. The Jacksons were a big family and most of them were grown and the neighborhood weren't about to let a bunch of bullies come in and intimidate one of their own so some of them joined in the fight as well. Brother his friends and Leah's other brother Martin fought off the seven or eight grown brothers in the Jackson clan and the Momma and her sisters including Anna fought off the women.

Eventually, someone called the police who responded and got peace by saying whoever did not leave the grass lot immediately was going to jail. Momma finally stopped fighting long enough to get her kids back to the house but when Martin walked into the house he spotted the stack of softball bats, grabbed one in each hand and bolted out of the back door. When he got to the end of the alley the police were there to greet him and he got arrested. That would be the first of many arrests for Martin.

Brother had gotten his gun and ran after Martin but when he saw the police he turned around and ran back with the police in hot pursuit. "He's got a gun!" one of the Jacksons yelled, but Brother beat the police back to the house ran in threw the gun into the closet and came back outside as if he had done no wrong. The police questioned him about having a gun but of course one of the sisters had hidden it by then. Brother offered to let the police search him and they did. Of course they didn't find the gun.

Leah's family spent the next month fighting the Jacksons almost everyday. The police were called everyday because someone, mostly the Jacksons would break the peace. Daddy, although he would show up to protect us, was gone for good by then so they thought that they would take advantage of a woman with a house full of girls and two teen-aged boys. They had no idea who they were taking on. Now Momma was trying to keep the peace, she didn't want her boys to go to jail so she tried to keep them calm. The Jacksons used every trick of intimidation known to them and eventually Momma got tired and called her brother.

When Uncle Man got there he and his business partner brought out automatic weapons and stood back to back in the grass lot declaring to the neighborhood that he would kill anyone who messed with his sister and her children. Later on that day after Uncle Man and his business partner left, two of the Jackson men rode down the street and threw bricks through the window at Leah's house. It was the beginning of the end for the Jacksons. The two brothers were arrested for breaking the peace bond and that left their families vulnerable. Later that night Leah saw a dark van parked down the street not far from the Jacksons house. It got her attention because it looked like the van that the cleaner's guy owned. This was a friend of her brothers'.

The van just sat there and no one got in or out of it. Later that night the Jacksons' home was on fire, the fire started at the back of the house and as they ran from the front of the house shots rang out. The bullets hit no one but needless to say Leah never saw the Jacksons again. The family did prepare for reprisals but none came, but nothing would ever be the same for Leah in that house after that summer.

CHAPTER FOUR

Leah started seventh grade that fall. Things were pretty good for her at school; she was an honor student and editor of the school newspaper. She had found a new love for reading and writing. She would imagine herself the heroine in the romance novels that she read taking herself to far off places in her mind. She read about places in London, Paris, the islands, and even in the United States that she didn't ever believe that she would visit. The more books she read, the more she wanted to read. She didn't want to be where she was anymore.

It was a constant party all the time with people in and out of the house. Momma would find a record that she liked and would play it over and over in an attempt to drown out the sorrow of Daddy leaving her for another woman. She had a new boyfriend but she was still in love with Daddy, which is probably the reason things didn't go very far with him She was very sad and did everything that she could to cover up her sadness. Mostly, she drank with her friends, played music and danced until she passed out.

Leah was also very sad about Daddy. He had finally admitted that not only was he not coming back, but that he had found another woman and wanted to marry her. Leah took it very hard and always wanted to be with her Daddy. Momma didn't like that one bit and so the fights started. Leah turned into the family martyr, she would either get blamed or take the blame for things that went wrong just to quiet Momma down. She really believed that Momma knew that she hadn't done most of the things that she had been accused of but she whooped her anyway. The belt, switches, and the extension cord were common occurrences in Leah's house. Not to mention a shoe or a book or whatever was handy when Momma got mad.

Leah remained an honor student in school but it was just about this time when the lies started. Momma had come to admit that she knew the other kids were using Leah for a scapegoat, so when Leah started doing things and then lying about Momma had a hard time at first telling what was true and what wasn't. Most of the other kids were doing things and getting away with it, or so Leah thought, and she was tired of being Miss goody two shoes. Besides it seemed to Leah that her wild sisters and brothers were not only getting all Mommas' attention, but she was also buying the things as well. Things Leah wasn't getting. She bought new clothes, skates, bikes as well as the fact that they always seemed to have money to buy the tings that they wanted.

Leah didn't understand why they were getting all of this attention, they were getting C's and D's in school and here she was a straight A student and getting no attention. Momma didn't come to her school events or support her on the newspaper as the other kids parents did. But if one of the others got into a fight or trouble Momma would be right there at school. It just wasn't fair. "Momma gone get you a bike before summer," she was told the year that her two older sisters got brand new bikes for Christmas, and "You don't even skate" she told her when they got the new skates. Leah once heard Momma tell one of her friends that she wasn't going up to the school for her as long as she was doing good because there was no need.

This was a very sad time for Leah. Even Anna wasn't paying her any attention anymore. She was busy preparing to join her husband in Florida. He had joined the Air Force and gotten stationed in Kissimmee right next to Disney World. Leah envied her sister so much, but she was very proud of the woman she had become. She was nothing like Momma, very caring and loving to her children. The only reason that Leah was sad about her leaving was that she would miss her terribly. She didn't realize that even with her three sisters that were older than she was she would have to step up and take over most of the responsibilities that Anna would leave behind.

Jean and Ina both had babies by now, and they couldn't take care of the things Momma and Pa-Pa needed taking care of. In fact Leah became a live in baby sitter as the girls continued to hang out sometimes leaving the babies home for Momma to take care of, which actually meant that Leah would be taking care of them. Leah wouldn't have minded that if they had even bothered to thank her but they thought that this is what she was supposed to be doing. She enjoyed her nieces and continued to take care of them until she found herself in another bad situation.

Since Anna had left Pa-Pa needed someone to go to his apartment through the week to do his laundry, and clean his apartment. Leah was so happy that she had been chosen to take over Anna's place with this job. It made her feel grown up to have the key to Pa Pa's house, catch the bus over there and wash and clean up there. It also made her feel good to finally have some money in her pocket to buy some of the things that she wanted. Pa-Pa would treat her special and always compared her to Anna. Little did she realize all of the duties she would have to take over for Anna.

Leah would go to the apartment and take Pa Pa's clothes down to the laundry room wash, dry and fold them. She would then go back to the apartment and pretend to be an adult on her own. It was a wonderful fantasy; too bad it would be sort lived. Leah looked forward to going to Pa Pa's apartment. Pa-Pa had a girlfriend who didn't live far from him.

One day when Leah got off the bus, she ran right into Violet who was on her way walking to Pa-Pa's house, so they walked together. They talked and laughed on the way. Violet told Leah that she had tried to call Pa-Pa and that nobody has answered the phone. When they got to the apartment, Violet put her key into the door and tried to open it but the chain was on the door. You could hear some kind of commotion going on in the apartment and finally Pa-Pa came and opened the door. They walked into the studio apartment. Pa-Pa was still adjusting his clothes and he wasn't alone. There was a young lady there with him and she had a very strange look on her face.

Violet immediately began to accuse Pa-Pa of messing around with the young lady but of course he denied it. Leah stood there embarrassed for both the young lady and Pa—Pa not knowing what to say or how to help diffuse the situation. Finally the young lady left and after a few rounds of accusations and denials, so did Violet. Leah could not believe what had just happened but she knew enough to know that Violet was right. Pa—Pa had been messing around with that young lady. How could he, she was not much older than Leah. In fact, as it would turn out, she and Anna were the same age and knew each other.

Leah tried to put it out of her mind but somewhere deep inside something she had not felt in years began to rise up. She did not want to feel it so she consciously pushed the thought away. Pa-Pa was a good man and he cared about her and her family a lot. They wouldn't be living in a beautiful new home and have some of the things that they had not to mention taking them places and doing things with them. She didn't want to believe that he could be a, "No," she pushed the thought away again. She started to think of the dinners where they would talk for hours and the hay rides on the back of his work trucks. She started to think about the fact that every time he came around he had something special for the kids. She thought about how good and grown up it made her feel to be in charge of cleaning his apartment and doing his laundry. Pa-Pa couldn't be a monster, could he? She made a conscious decision not to believe it; it would not be long before she regretted that decision.

Pa-Pa called one Sunday morning to say that he was on his way to pick up whoever wanted to go to church with him. Leah loved to go to church, she enjoyed the singing and preaching and the fact that Pa-Pa was a very important man in the church. Being the granddaughter of the head deacon was a very impressive thing back then. Leah loved it when they would call on Pa-Pa to pray. It was an amazing thing to see. This particular Sunday no one would want to go with him except Leah.

The service was beautiful as usual. Instead of going back to Pa-Pa's apartment to cook they stopped and got hamburgers, Leah's favorite. The two of them took the hamburgers back to the apartment, set the table and ate them. Pa-Pa was acting very strange but Leah thought it had something to do with church business or the sermon that had been preached that day. She went about cleaning up the few dishes that they had used. She immediately felt uncomfortable when Pa-Pa rubbed her back as she passed him to put away the dishes.

That feeling was back, that sick kind of fear that made Leah want to puke. She was paralyzed with fear when Pa-Pa pulled her down onto his lap to tell her how proud he was of the woman that she was becoming. He began to stroke her hair and kiss her in a way that men shouldn't kiss young girls. She was absolutely frozen with fear. She wanted to scream but no sound would come, who would hear her anyway. Her mind went back momentarily to the day that she and Violet had caught him with that young girl. She desperately wanted this to be a bad joke or a nightmare.

Pa-Pa continued to touch her, now in places that he had no business touching. "Nooo," she finally heard herself say, "Shhh," Pa-Pa told her, "This is going to make you a woman, and everything is going to be alright." But it wasn't all right; in fact there was nothing right about it. She felt the tears running down her cheek, she heard herself crying, "No, No, No," but he wasn't listening. She tried to struggle a loose, but he only held on tighter. Somehow she managed to open her eyes and when she did she wished that she hadn't.

Leah immediately began to scream and cry, while Pa-Pa held her down until he was done. As much as she did not want to believe it there was more than one monster, Pa-Pa was a monster too. Something in her changed that day; it would be years before she could figure out exactly what it was. One thing was for sure, she could not go back to being that care free teenager that left the house this morning excited about going to church. In fact it would be a long time before she was ever excited about anything again.

She didn't understand how he could say that he loved her and even better than that, loved God, and be able to do this to young girls. She didn't understand how God could let this happen to her. He was supposed to love her, they both were. Was this how you showed people that you loved them? Leah had been exposed to so much and yet she still didn't understand about sex. Worst than that, she didn't have anyone that she could ask. The one person that she might be able to tell this too was miles away. The thought occurred to her, "Did he do this to Anna?" It would explain why right before Anna left for Florida, she made Leah or somebody would go with her to Pa-Pa's every time. It would make sense that she wouldn't want to be alone with him.

Leah struggled in her mind the rest of the afternoon. Pa-Pa went about his business watching the baseball game as if nothing had happened. She was so confused, how could anyone do this to his own granddaughter? There was only one answer that she could come up with in her mind. Pa-Pa didn't care about her; nobody did, not Momma, not Daddy, not even Anna. How could they? Momma would be mad at her if she told she knew that. She might not even believe her. Daddy couldn't care or he wouldn't have left her there with Momma to go and help another woman raise her daughters, and if Anna cared, she would have warned her about Pa-Pa.

Maybe this was the way that things were supposed to be. Maybe, as she had begun to think earlier, this was the way that people showed how they loved each other. How in her thirteen year-old mind was she supposed to figure this out for herself? Momma had figured it out for herself at this age. By the time that Momma was fourteen years old she'd had a baby and gotten married. Maybe she should just stop complaining and try to be grown-up about the situation. There was really no other choice for her. She couldn't tell, she had seen Momma get mad at people and she sure didn't want to be on the receiving end of that if she could help it.

Leah had made up her mind by the time she left Pa-Pa's that day. She wouldn't tell. Not only would she not tell but she had also made up in her mind that this was the way things were supposed to be. The only time that things turned out differently for families was on T.V. or in the many books that she read. More than ever she was convinced that that she was supposed to follow in her mother's footsteps.

CHAPTER FIVE

School became less and less important to Leah. Even though she was very smart, a straight A student at the time she dreaded going to school. She knew that she was different from the other kids and she was afraid that they could recognize it too. Not only was she considered overweight and had protruding teeth from sucking her thumb, she had gone from elementary and junior high, where she was at the top of her class, to high school, which required a lot more study and preparation, but she had no idea how to get the results that she desired and no one to show her how. Momma couldn't show her, she didn't know how. Momma's answer to every situation was to beat Leah. High school graduates were unheard of in her family. In fact her sister Lynn would be the first one in the family to ever graduate from high school.

The fact that she had always been a wiz at school, and that she no longer was only added to her dilemma. She wasn't good at anything anymore. She wasn't worth anything, except maybe the fact that men wanted to sleep with her. Is that all that she was worth? She started to skip school. Momma's beatings became more and more frequent. She would use her key to Pa-Pa's apartment to go and hide out during school hours. Then she would go back home and act as if everything was O.K. She had never been in trouble at school before so she was able to fool everyone for a while. It wouldn't be long before all of her lies began to catch up with her.

Leah was watching T.V. one day when she heard about a new medical condition scientist had discovered. She had been skipping school so regularly that her counselor had sent a letter home stating that she wanted a conference with her parents. Of course Leah had gotten a hold to the letter before her Momma saw it. Knowing that if Momma talked to the counselor she would find out about her skipping school, she made an elaborate story about having this degenerative eye condition. She called the counselor and pretended to be Momma. Somehow, the counselor fell for it but only for a while. By the end of the school year, the truth came out about Leah skipping school and the fact that she was failing.

She was devastated; Momma was more upset than she had ever been with Leah. She beat her for what seemed like hours with an extension cord. She had so many welts and bruises on her she could hardly walk. Somebody called and told Daddy but when he found out what Leah had done he didn't have very much sympathy for her. Momma was fed up, she didn't have time to deal with Leah's problems she had problems of her own. She packed Leah up and sent her to stay with Anna for the summer who by then was closer to home in Dayton, Ohio.

Leah felt thrown away, here she was on a Greyhound bus headed for Ohio all alone. Of course it made her feel good when the handsome man asked her to sit next to him on the bus ride to "keep him company." By now Leah was not naïve about sexual matters. She knew what the man wanted and she had no intentions of giving into him. She did however want to be in the company of a handsome man on a long bus ride so she sat next to him to play along acting as if she didn't know what he wanted. It wasn't long before he made his move. Halfway to Dayton in a little town called Lima the man decided that it was a perfect time to make his move.

It was the middle of the night and everyone was asleep, or so he thought. Leah was half dozing when she felt him touch her breast. She immediately woke up to him with a big stupid grin on his face. "Shh" he said to her, "Everyone is sleeping," he said as he tried to reach under Leah's shirt. "No wait," she said as she sat straight up in her seat, "I think I'd better go to the bathroom," she said louder than she intended to. Leah got up and made a beeline for the bathroom. On her way past a woman looked up from her seat and gave Leah a look that she didn't quite understand, she kept going past the woman to the bathroom. She didn't know what to do. She stood in the bathroom for what seemed like forever afraid to move or make a sound. She knew that it would be at least a couple of more hours before they got to Dayton and she couldn't stay in the bathroom forever. "What am I going to do now?" she asked herself. She couldn't make a scene, everybody had saw her and the man together laughing and talking, and she had let him buy her dinner knowing full well what he wanted in return.

Just then someone knocked on the door startling her. "I'll be right out," she barely said. She half expected to open the door and see the man standing there but it wasn't him. There was a lady with her kid that needed to use the bathroom. She came out of the bathroom but didn't move forward. She stepped aside enough for the lady and her kid to get into the bathroom. She was trying to plot out her next move in her head when the woman that she had passed earlier looked up and said quietly, "This seat is not taken." Now Leah recognized the look, it was sympathy and she sure was glad to see it. She scooted past the woman and took the window seat quickly. The woman gave her a shawl to cover herself with and she did just that, eyes and all.

She peeked from under the shawl after a few minutes and then she really understood. From where the woman sat she had a perfect view of the seat Leah and the stranger shared. She had seen everything and now Leah could peek from under the shawl, look between the seats and see him twisting and turning in his chair, trying to see what had happened to Leah. When he saw the woman and her child come out of the bathroom he got up and headed for the back of the bus. The bus was very dark and cold and everyone was covered up. The woman didn't even look up from her reading but he had the nerve to ask her anyway. "Did you see that young lady that I was with earlier come out of the bathroom?" "Evidently," the woman said, "She ain't trying to see you." He was ticked off but went back to his seat.

The woman never looked at Leah as she explained that she had seen everything from the beginning. She said that she knew that Leah was too young to be hooking up with this man on a bus ride. She told her that she reminded her of her granddaughter and she wasn't about to let anything happen to her, "That is if you want my help" the woman said. Leah never agreed to anything so fast in her life, but she also stayed quiet and hidden under the shawl until they reached Dayton.

The woman stood up to take her things down from the top of the bus, the man looked back but still didn't see Leah so he got off the bus. When he walked away Leah thanked the woman ran to her former seat grabbed her things from up top and got off the bus. She was never so happy to see her sister and brother-in-law, as she was that day. She almost ran and jumped into Anna's arms. Again Anna had turned out to be her hero, or was she. Just as she picked up her stored suitcases she looked to her left and there was the stranger. She literally stopped breathing for a minute until her brother-in-law stepped up to grab the suitcase. Once the man saw the uniformed soldier he decided against any trouble and didn't say a word. The three of them headed to their car with Anna holding her breath the whole time afraid of what the man might do or say. She was afraid for nothing because the man went about his business and never said a word.

This was sort of a bittersweet reunion for the sisters who had missed each other so much. Anna was very happy to see her sister and even happy to catch a break with the cost of daycare, but she really didn't have room for a teenaged sister who thought she was grown. She and her husband Gary were going through a very tough time financially. There was just more bills than money and they simply did not think that they could afford to take care of Leah. Somehow, things worked out for Leah that summer and she was able to stay with Anna and her husband for the summer.

It turned out to be a carefree summer for Leah. She had made so much trouble for herself lately that Dayton had become a welcome change. Anna and Gary had lots of friends and they socialized quite a bit together. Leah made new friends of her own, all of them older than she was and began to socialize with them separately. Because they were older than she was they could legally drink and as Leah began to hang around them she began to drink with them. Soon she realized that all of the hurt and fear that she felt on a daily basis would disappear when she drank so she began to drink more.

They had lots of what she thought was fun that summer, parties, hanging out at the NCO club and traveling. Leah was only fifteen years old now but she could get into any club because she looked and acted so mature, not to mention the fact that she was always with people that were older than she was. One thing she began to realize was that no matter how many people were around she still always felt alone. But feeling alone in a crowd was better than actually being alone so she continued to hang out with her newfound friends and to drink with them.

The summer was over much to fast for Leah, now she had to go back home and pretend to fit in with the other fifteen year olds at her school. Momma had moved into another new house by then and what should have been a new beginning for Leah didn't quite turn out that way.

CHAPTER SIX

Leah went back to high school and began to try to put her life back on track. However she was very uncomfortable there for at least a couple of reasons. First of all she still had the same counselor as before. They had allowed her to do some make-up work so that she would pass the ninth grade, but this woman was now watching her like a hawk. Secondly, the school that Leah attended was for high achievers and although she really was smart, she had missed so much in ninth grade that the other kids were flying past her in their work and that only served to send her self esteem, (already in the basement) to a new low. She remembered how drinking had made her feel so began drinking just not to feel the shame and embarrassment of not (she thought) being able to cut it at school.

The only way that she was able to drink was to hang around people that did, so she began hanging out with her friends and cousins that did, sometimes she would go places and stay too long, she would then be afraid to go home either because she had too much to drink or she was afraid to get into trouble for staying out late. Hence the run a ways started. When she would finally make it home Momma would nearly beat the skin off of her and tell her that the only place that she was allowed to go was to school. By now, school was the last place that Leah wanted to be, so the minute she left the house in the mornings she would find someplace to go other than school. That's how she ended up hooking up with Jamie.

Jamie was the grandson of Brother's girlfriend. He was just a couple of years older than Leah, which was a first for her because up until then the only men interested in Leah were much older. Jamie was handsome, he was the star tight end for his school, which rivaled and usually beat Leah's school and he didn't live far from Daddy and his new wife. Leah thought that the sun rose and set in this boy's eyes and she would do absolutely anything to be with him. The only problem was Jamie had a girlfriend. Leah did have an advantage over the girlfriend in that Jamie's grandmother hated the girlfriend and really took a liking to Leah.

Jamie's grandmother, Fanny, was not like any grandmother Leah had ever known. In fact his whole family was different than any that she had ever known. Leah thought that it was great that they were so close. His mom, Mary supported him in everything that he did and was very proud of him. Jamie didn't drink or use other drugs, but he could have. Mary was a firm believer in allowing her kids to get high at home so that they wouldn't do it out in the streets but Jamie was a true athlete and wouldn't put drugs of any kind into his body.

For the next few months Leah and Jamie snuck around seeing each other when his girlfriend wasn't around. She began to visit her Daddy and his wife more and more not only because she was in trouble at home but also Jamie lived close and could walk to her Daddy's house. Of course the only thing Leah thought that she had to offer him was sex and that is what they did on a regular basis. Leah absolutely loved being with Jamie. She didn't ever want to not be with him so she did whatever she had to do to be with him. She was barely going to school and barely passing but she didn't care, she just wanted to be with Jamie. All this time though they were still sneaking around. He kept telling her that he was going to tell his girl about them but he hadn't. It became a very uncomfortable situation for Leah who had to play second when the girl was around.

It became more and more obvious that they belonged together and his Mom and Granny (as Jamie called her) encouraged him to break up with the other girl. The young lady was crazy about Jamie and was not going to go away easily. One night at a party at Fanny's house the girl, (who was already suspicious of Leah and Jamie) confronted Leah. Leah told her that she had nothing to say to her and that if she had any questions then she should ask Jamie. She screamed at Leah to stay away from him but Leah told her that wasn't her decision to make and that she should talk to Jamie.

She did and when he admitted that she had been seeing Leah, the girl lost it, pulled a knife and came after Leah. Jamie was able to stop her but the drama that would begin that night would send Leah's life into a tailspin. Brother and Jamie escorted her from the party. Jamie said that he was just going to calm her down and that he would be back. After a while Brother came back but Jamie didn't. Leah was afraid now. The girl had threatened to kill her and Jamie and he wasn't back. She tried to be brave but she knew that something wasn't right.

The party was still going strong when Brother came back. Everybody was still dancing, laughing and talking about what had just happened. Brother made his way over to Leah, "Are you o.k.?" he asked, "She didn't cut you did she?" "No," Leah answered, "Where is Jamie?" "He's still talking to Tammy, he'll be back in a few minutes," he answered, then asked again, "Are you sure you're o.k.?" "Yes" she answered, and walked away. Brother watched her from across the room. Leah believed that he was truly concerned but she still couldn't get past what he had done to her as a little girl. It just felt uncomfortable being in his presence one on one and even more uncomfortable for him to be concerned about her.

"Jamie, what's up?" she heard someone ask shaking her out of her thoughts. "Everything is cool" he said as he began to walk toward Leah. He was purposely trying to make eye contact with her as if he was trying to look down into her soul. For the first time since she had started to see Jamie she felt a little guilty and she couldn't hold his gaze. "Are you o.k.?" he asked. "Yes" she said irritated that everyone kept asking her that. "Where is Tammy is she O.K.?" Leah asked. "I took her home and I guess she is as well as can be expected," Jamie answered. "What does that mean?" Leah asked him. "Come on let's go someplace where we can talk privately," he answered. Leah didn't like the sound of that response but she would follow Jamie anywhere and so she did.

They went outside on the porch; Jamie grabbed Leah and hugged her tightly letting out a deep sigh. Then he took another deep breath pulled her away and looked at her asking her again if she was o.k. She assured him that she was and they sat down to talk. He told her how he really felt bad for cheating on Tammy but that he wasn't sorry that he did. He assured her that it felt just as right to him as it did to her when they were together but that he wished that he hadn't hurt Tammy the way that he did. Leah really felt guilty now.

He went on to say that he wished that the two of them could spend the rest of their lives together but that because of what Tammy had told him tonight that would not be possible. She was pregnant. Leah didn't hear much else he said after that, she felt something close to panic rise up in her and she had to fight the urge to pass out. She felt the urge to throw up, her head was spinning; she bent down and put her head between her legs and took several deep breaths. When she could hear him again he was saying, "I'm not sure whether or not to believe her but if it's true, I can't leave her now." He hadn't even realized that Leah had zoned out for a few minutes. She told herself that she shouldn't have had so much to drink at the party.

She was afraid to open her mouth because she wasn't sure what was going to come out. She wasn't sure if she would vomit, scream, cry or tell him that she understood. She did understand the concept that if Tammy was pregnant that he would want to stay with her but she didn't want that to be what he was saying. She wanted him to say that it didn't matter if she was pregnant or not that he wanted to be with her no matter what, but if he said that it would make him one of them "no good neggahs" Momma was always calling her sisters babies fathers.

The only thing that could help her out of this situation would be if it just weren't true. She had to hold on to that possibility. Jamie was asking her if she understood and she wasn't answering him so he asked her again. She could only nod yes before the tears started coming. She couldn't identify the feelings that she was experiencing but it was perhaps the deepest hurt that she had ever felt. Jamie reached over to her and held her and they both cried.

Leah didn't want to make Jamie feel any worse than he already felt. She wanted to stop crying but she couldn't. The pain was if someone had reached in and snatched out her heart. She had been hurt before but this was something she couldn't even identify. She felt physically ill, her head pounded and she really did want to vomit. "Oh God, Oh God, Oh God" was all that she could say. She would much rather face the monster than feel this kind of pain. Jamie was caught in the middle, not only did he feel the pain of the two young women but his own as well. It would not be easy to give up his dreams of college and a shot at the pros, but he would have to man up and handle this situation.

Leah and Jamie must have talked for hours about what they were going to do. Jamie told Leah that he didn't want it to be true and shared all of his reasons. His entire life had just changed in one night. He thought that this would be the night when he would tell Tammie the truth and get on with his life. His life that included playing ball for one of the schools that was trying to recruit him. At the very least he would get a free ride to pay for his college education. He had been so careful to protect his education and football career. He had kept his grades up, stayed out of the streets, didn't use drugs or get into trouble in school. His life as he knew it was over.

By the time they were done talking that night Leah felt worse for Jamie than she felt for herself. They promised to stay friends no matter what happened with Tammy, but they would not stay together if she was pregnant. Leah just couldn't go through that. They would both get on with their education and their lives. Jamie made Leah promise that she would go back and really try to get her head back in school and get along with her Momma. Leah made the promise but she would not be able to keep it.

CHAPTER SEVEN

Leah didn't last two weeks at her Mom's house. Things were so messed up at home and at school that it was very hard for her to face the mess that she had made of her life. She didn't begin to know how to fix it and all her mother could do was to say, "I told you so" and ridicule Leah for the choices that she had made. It was the holiday season but Leah wasn't feeling very festive. The only good thing about it being the holiday season was that Momma constantly had friends over for drinks. Leah was able to drink on a regular basis for those two weeks that she was home with her Momma. She drank so much that the entire two weeks were mostly a blur. Momma pretended not to know that she was drinking and jumped at the chance to send her to stay with her Daddy for the holiday season.

Daddy had planned a trip up north to the cabins that his wife's family owned. Leah's stepfamily was pretty cool. Her step-mom Shari was very concerned about Leah and what she was going through. She sat Leah down to give her "the talk" about boys and all that they wanted, a talk that had never come from her mother. She did her best to encourage Leah to get herself together. Leah was trying but every time she let herself think about the situation, she could feel herself actually getting physically ill and she would find a way to get another drink. Drinks were plentiful at Daddy's house also, he never went too many days without having a drink.

Leah's stepsister Sandy decided to take matters into her own hands when she couldn't get Leah out of her funk. On Thanksgiving Day, Daddy and Shari had lots of company over. Leah and Sandy spent the day helping Shari prepare dinner and Sandy had made a date for Leah for later that night. Daddy said that it would be O.K., everybody thought that it would be a good idea for Leah and Sandy to go out on a double date so that she could try to forget about Jamie. Leah agreed.

When it was time the guys showed up to pick them up. By this point everyone in the house had been drinking so nobody paid any attention to them as they left the house. Leah was excited to be going on a real date; her date was the driver so she felt really grown up. They didn't have a particular destination so they drove to Belle Isle and drove around the park. The water fountain was beautifully lit up so they decided to park there. While they were parked there, Sandy's date pulled out a crazy water pipe. "Yeah, that's what I'm talking about," Sandy said. "What the heck is that?" Leah asked them. "It's a weed pipe," her date answered. Leah had been drinking for quite sometime and she had been places with Jamie where they were smoking weed but he would never let her smoke any. She was a little bit afraid so she said she wouldn't do it. The guys and Sandy started to tease her so she said to Sandy, "Jamie would kill me if he found out that I smoked this stuff." "You are so stupid" Sandy told Leah, "That boy is somewhere with Tammy and he ain't thinking about you or what you doing."

What Sandy said hurt really bad, but it was the truth Leah thought. Jamie was somewhere spending the holidays with Tammy preparing to have their baby. The mental picture was far too much for her to handle so she changed her mind and accepted the weed pipe from the young man. She took a couple of tokes and nothing happened. They passed the pipe around the car and when it came back to Leah she took it again. They passed it around several more times and on the last time Leah got choked.

She thought that it would stop and that she would be able to catch her breath but it didn't. She kept coughing trying her best to force down air into her windpipe but it just would not happen. The other teenagers in the car began to panic. Sandy started to pat her on the back and somehow it allowed a breath of air to go into her lung. It took a few minutes but Leah was able to get her normal breathing rhythm back, but she could hardly talk. All of a sudden everything became so funny to her.

It didn't matter that she had just nearly died, everything and everyone that she looked at appeared to her as some life-sized cartoon. She could not stop laughing no matter how hard she tried, and she was desperately trying. Sandy and the two boys were panicking by now. One of the boys suggested that they get her something to eat "Maybe that will calm her down" her date said, "If I take her home like this, your Dad is going to kill me!" he told Sandy. They all agreed that the food would help, Leah was still laughing uncontrollably when they got to the restaurant. The boys took their orders and got out of the car to go inside, Leah remembered that she had not ordered anything to drink and tried to let down the window to tell her date.

The windows were electric and the car was turned off so Leah attempted to open the door to tell the boys to bring her a drink but the door would not open. Again she began to laugh uncontrollably. This time it was serious, she could not breathe and she knew that she needed some air. She turned around to tell Sandy that she needed some air but the words wouldn't come out, only hysterical laughing. She really needed some air but not only did Sandy not understand how desperately she needed to open the door and get some air, but she was busy laughing herself and desperately holding down the lock so that Leah couldn't get out of the car.

Leah's hysterical laughs turned into a desperate cry but her sister was not about to let her get out of the car. She was afraid that someone would see how Leah was acting, know that she was high and that they would get into trouble. Sandy was determined not to do the very thing that Leah felt would save her life at this moment, so she held on tight to the door lock. She had no way of knowing how desperately Leah needed air and Leah couldn't tell her. Minutes seemed like hours but finally the boys came back with their order and opened the door. Leah took this opportunity to jump out of the car. Sandy jumped out right behind her but Leah didn't run as Sandy thought that she would, she just laid on the hood of the car gasping for air and crying.

The cries came from deep within. Leah had never experienced anything like this before. The tears just would not stop coming. It was as if someone had opened a floodgate or a dam and the tears and emotions had just come rushing out with no way to stop them. All Sandy could do was stand there with her and hold her while she cried. Leah felt so stupid for taking the drugs, for getting involved with Jamie, for letting Brother and Pa-Pa have her, hey, where were these feeling coming from? She didn't know and she could not stop them.

Thank God the boys thought it was just the weed. They had no idea of the emotional roller coaster ride that Leah had been on. They felt really guilty about giving Leah the drugs so they stayed with the girls until the waves of emotions stopped. Leah was limp when it was all over. The boys insisted that Leah eat the food they had gone to get. Just then it dawned on Leah that she had not told anyone what had just happened. When she began to explain it actually was kind of funny, especially the part about Sandy holding down the lock but Leah wasn't about to start laughing again, she was afraid, she told them that it would be a long time, if ever before she laughed again.

Leah and Sandy went into the bathroom at the restaurant; they ignored all of the stares and strange looks that they had gotten on the way in. When they looked in the mirror they understood what the people were looking at. They looked horrible, red puffy eyes, their hair all over their head, and just a wild look in general about them. They both burst out laughing when they looked in the mirror.

This time it was Sandy who started to cry, not as Leah had cried earlier but still tears of sadness and fear. There would be no way to hide the way that they looked when they got home and she knew that Shari and Daddy would hold her responsible for what had happened. When she shared her fears with Leah she vowed to take the blame for herself. It was not Sandy's fault they she was stupid enough not only to take the drugs, but to take too much of it. They wondered if the boys were still outside waiting for them. They joked that if they were boys they would have left themselves by now. It was time for them to go home and face the music. The boys drove them home; they got out of the car afraid to go in but happy to be able to. They stepped into the house, which was full of music and talking. Everyone had continued to drink while they were gone. The girls were home early and after a brief hello to everyone they ran upstairs to Sandy's room. No one had noticed that the girls were high, or so they thought. Shari came up later to check on them and although she couldn't quite figure out what they had done she knew they had done something, but she let them sleep. They had dodged the bullet.

CHAPTER EIGHT

The next morning they packed up and left for the cabins. Leah was tired and hung over and was looking forward to making it up north to get some rest. She had no idea that the cabins were not the place to go if you wanted to get some rest. The only rest that she would get that entire weekend would be on the drive up and back. She had never been on a real vacation before and she had no idea how much she would enjoy this weekend.

As soon as they got there Leah was introduced to Auntie. Auntie was a statuesque older woman who must have been drop dead gorgeous in her day. Today she appeared matronly and stern. Leah was shown the "kids cabin" which was about 1000 ft. from where the grown-ups partied and was told that they could go anywhere in the small resort town that they wanted as long as they did not miss 10:00 bed check. She was shown how to put coals in the stove and told what time to do so. Auntie warned her not to let the fire go all the way out or they would not start it again until the next day. After receiving all of the necessary instruction, Sandy and Leah took off into the woods.

The first place that Sandy took her to was a place called "The Spot." It was where all the young people gathered to listen to music, dance, eat, and just hang out. The Spot was full of teenagers when they got there. In the background the Commodores sang about being a brick house while Sandy introduced Leah to all of her friends. The atmosphere was charged with laughter and dancing and it wasn't long before Leah felt comfortable with all of her new friends. Friends who had known each other nearly since birth a concept that made her a little uncomfortable, but they accepted her and so she began to dance and enjoy herself. They left "The Spot" and went to a friend's house to play cards and continue listening to music. They were having so much fun when Sandy announced that it was time to get back to the "kid's cabin" before bed check at 10:00 p.m.

Leah hated it but she went along with it any way. It seemed that all the teenagers had a 10:00 bed check. What seemed to be the designated leaders of the group stood off to the side and whispered. When Sandy got to Leah she asked her what they were whispering about. Sandy told her not to worry about it, that she would know when the time came and they left.

Sandy led Leah back to the cabin through the woods. She told Leah to stay close because there were no street lights and she didn't want her to get lost. She didn't have to say it twice because it was very dark, not to mention the fact that Leah had never spent any time in the country. As they got closer to the cabins they could hear the music coming from the adults cabin. Along with the music was loud laughing and talking. The adults were in the middle of a Thanksgiving weekend party with no end in sight. Sandy seemed pleased at this fact and Leah just thought that she was happy to see her parents having a good time. She had no way of knowing the reasoning behind the smile that was on her face.

They got to the cabin just in time to put the coals in the coal stove so that the fire would not go out. It was still pretty cold so they slept in their socks, hats, and gloves. All of these things would work together to make this one of the most memorable nights of her young life. It was exactly 10:00 when Auntie stuck her head into the cabin and yelled, "Bed Check." They all laughed as Auntie made mention that they had barely made it in time. Leah hopped into bed and pulled the cover up over her head.

Leah felt as if she had just dozed off to sleep when Sandy began shaking her. She opened her eyes and tried to adjust them to the dark. "Shhh," she heard Sandy say, "Get up and follow me." "Where are we going?" Leah asked. "Shhh, don't worry about it," Sandy told her, "Just follow me." Leah did just that, she watched as Sandy stuffed her bed with pillows and did the same. "We sneaking out?" Leah asked. "Don't worry about it just hurry up." Leah hurried to finish stuffing her bed giggling the whole time. When they were finished Leah followed Sandy to out of the door and into the woods. When they were a good distance away they both burst out laughing. They had gotten away!

The girls met up at a prearranged spot with all the rest of the kids that had managed to sneak out. They were all laughing and talking about how they had tricked their parents into getting back out. It was a continuation party; everybody seemed to pick up where they had left off. Some guys showed up on their snowmobiles. They all looked real fly in their helmets and snowmobile suits. Sandy introduced Leah to Mike who seemed to like Leah right away. They began to talk and to get to know each other. They were partners in the card game and seemed to be very comfortable with each other. All the while the other guys were racing through the woods in the dark showing off their skills, or their stupidity as it would turn out. They seemed to be having so much fun.

Mike asked if she had ever been on a "machine," as he called his snowmobile. He had raced a couple of times that night with some luck. He had won a couple, lost a couple. When Leah admitted that she had never ridden he said, "Tonight is your lucky night." He grabbed Leah by the hand and walked her over to the snowmobile. He gave her a helmet and a few basic instructions on leaning into the turns. As soon as he revved up his engine someone challenged him by pulling up next to him and revving their engine. Someone counted off, on the mark, get set, go!

Off they went through the dark woods, around curves and in between trees. Leah was scared, she wanted this ride to be over quickly but it was not so. They would race around the entire lake before stopping. Mike had a good lead on the other couple but these guys did not believe in losing. Just as Mike was about to take the last curve in the dark woods the other couple came from out of nowhere and cut them off. Leah remembered hitting mailbox after mailbox before the snowmobile finally went down. Mike tried to hold on but he could not. Leah actually jumped before the machine hit the ground. Mike was still holding onto his machine when it hit the ground with a thud and slid away from him. "My Machine!" Leah heard him say as the rest of the crowd began to scream. She was half dazed but even in that she could not believe that he had almost killed them and wasn't worried about her or himself, only his stupid "machine"

Leah was banged up, the snowmobile suit and helmet had served its purpose. She wasn't scraped at all but she was a little hurt. Mike on the other hand had really hurt himself trying to hold on to the snowmobile. His suit was torn and he was scraped up bad on his arms. He said something to her about leaning the wrong way but she barely heard him before she passed out.

Someone took her into a cabin and put some smelling salts to her nose. This brought her around quickly but when she tried to sit up she could hardly move. Somewhere in the background she could still hear the young man complaining about his snowmobile. This just made her want to get up even more so that she could tell him off. His desire to win had just nearly killed her, and the desire to save his "machine" had just nearly killed him. Sandy was on the same page as Leah, she was angry as hell that this idiot had just nearly killed her sister. She was also scared to death that her parents would have to find out that they had snuck out.

Leah groaned and Sandy snapped out of her deep thought. "Are you alright?" she asked her sister. "I don't think anything is broken, but everything hurts," Leah answered her as she started to cry. Now Sandy was really mad, she had watched the entire race and if Mike had not been so hell bent on winning the race he could have let the other riders pass and this would not have happened. "I told her to lean with me," she heard him say before she decided she had heard just about enough of his stupid arrogant mouth. "You IDIOT!" she yelled at him, "All you had to do was slow down and let them pass." "What are you talking about slow down, it was a race!" he yelled back. "Not to the death!" she fired back,

Just then the cabin door opened and a huge man walked in. Sandy looked as if she had seen a ghost, but the surprise on her face immediately turned to relief. She flew across the room and jumped into his arms. "Louie!" was all Leah heard her sister say. She ran into his arms and held on tight. He wrapped his never ending arms around her and told her that everything would be O.K., he would take care of everything he assured her. He glared at Mike, "I know that I did not just hear you yelling at my niece?" Louie asked him. "I am so sorry" he quickly apologized.

Leah was still kind of dazed as she watched the whole exchange. Louie looked down at Sandy and asked her what happened. She started to explain and Mike interrupted her. "Man if you do not shut up," Louie warned. Sandy went on with her story, when she got to the part of the story about the other riders cutting Mike off and Mike not slowing down, he glared at Mike once again. "Man I'm sorry," Mike said again. You very well may be before this night is over. Louie walked over to Leah; he knelt down to take a closer look at her. Leah had never seen this man before yet he looked so familiar. He asked her questions and she answered him, she couldn't believe that someone she didn't even know would be so concerned about her.

Sandy walked over to them, "Louie, we snuck out." "No kidding" he said back to her sarcastically. Sandy and Leah began to cry. If this grown up knew, surely Daddy and Shari would find out and they would be in big trouble. "Can you sit up?" Louie asked her. She tried and was successful. Louie helped her to her feet and over to a chair. He told someone to get her some water as he went about taking off her boots and checking out her feet, legs, and ankles. It was at this point he looked up at her asked, "Do you know who I am?" softly enough so that only she could hear him. Leah just shook her head no and Louie went on to tell her that he was her Uncle Louie, Shari's younger brother and that if she wanted him to he would go over and bash Mike's head in for her.

Leah did not want that, so she just shook her head no. Louie had to be the most gorgeous man that she had ever seen in her young life. Six feet six inches tall and about 240 lbs., his arms weren't like any she had ever seen. They were long and muscular with giant hands at the end of them. His skin was caramel colored and flawless and he sported a big mustache. He had beautiful light brown eyes and the most gorgeous smile Leah had ever seen. The best part about all of this was that he was there to take care of Leah and her sister. He helped her zip her boots back up and stood up. "WOW!" she thought to herself when he stood directly in front of her.

He walked toward Mike who immediately stood and started to back up. Everyone thought that he would hit him for sure, but he just reached out and put one of his gigantic hands around Mike's neck. "If you ever put any body that belongs to me on the back of one of your machines I will personally bury you and your machine, are we clear?" Louie glared at him one last time before letting him go. "Yeah. Man I'm sorry!" Mike answered back. "You can go home and tell your parents that if anything is really wrong with my niece they can be prepared to pay for the doctor!" Mike just hung his head and nodded yes. Louie turned to Sandy who was still crying, partially because she was scared of her parents finding out about them sneaking out but mostly because she had watched the race and she just knew that Leah had to be hurt.

Leah wasn't crying anymore, not that she wasn't hurt or scared, but the pride that she felt at that moment over rode the fear and the pain. This was all new to her. Sandy and all the other kids were not very surprised by the way Louie came in and handled the situation. In fact she heard one of the teenagers say that she thought that Louie would kill Mike for sure. Leah had never experienced this kind of protection from the men in her family, even

Daddy had never been willing to fight for her, except of course with Momma. She was overwhelmed with pride. Louie looked over at her and her sister, "Don't move," he told Leah, "I'm going to get the car and I'll be back," he told them both as he left out of the door. Soon after he went out of the door Leah heard what she had come to learn all to quickly was the sound of a snow mobile speeding off. Mike took that moment to apologize one last time and head for the hills. None of the teenagers that were left in the cabin knew what to say. They were pretty much reserved to the fact that they would all be grounded for the rest of the weekend when their parents found out.

But Louie didn't tell, he came back and got the girls as he had promised and drove them the short distance to the cabin where they were supposed to be sleeping. The lights were still on in the big cabin and Leah instantly felt a lump in her throat. It was just before dawn and way past the time when they were supposed to have put coals on the fire. Louie parked the car on the road and they began to walk to the cabin. They could still hear music and laughter coming from the big house. Leah could not believe that they were going to get away with this too.

They approached the cabin quietly; Louie motioned for them to go inside. They got inside quickly but immediately wanted to go back outside. The fire had long since gone out and it was colder inside the cabin than it was outside. Bone chilling cold and Leah immediately began to shiver. You could see your own breath in the cabin it was so cold. Louie went right into action to get the fire started. She wanted to sleep in her clothes, but Sandy made her get into her pajamas. Once Louie got the fire started he hugged them both and eased out of the cabin. Somewhere in the distance she heard the car motor start, but by then she was snuggled under the cover and almost asleep. The last thought that crossed her mind was that if she never heard another motor in her life it would be to soon, and then she fell asleep.

It was the best sleep that she had in quite some time. The combination of cold air, activity, and the drinks they had the night before was working together perfectly for her to be able to sleep. It would be days before she realized she had hardly thought about Jamie at all. The sleep was just getting good when Auntie opened the cabin door and declared that it was time to get up. "You all must have gotten up this morning and added more coals to the fire, I was sure it would be cold in here by now" she talked mostly to herself as she went about straightening the cabin. Leah just smiled to herself as she remembered the events from last night. Again they had dodged the bullet this time with the help of her new hero.

CHAPTER NINE

She was instantly crazy about Louie as was everyone that he met. It wasn't the kind of "crazy about" that Leah was used to feeling when it came to men. It was sort of the crazy about that she felt about her Daddy. The feelings were very mutual; Louie treated Leah as if he had known her all of her life. They would share secret smiles for a long time to come.

Leah and Sandy got up and helped Auntie clean and prepare breakfast. The "grown folks" were still sleeping because it had not been to long since they had gone to bed. This was all a new experience for Leah; she had never in her mind experienced this kind of family closeness. Doing things together, having fun together, getting in trouble together, these were things that were all new to her. She had been so alone for so long. She was about to start crying when Daddy walked into the room and said good morning to her. "Hey Daddy" she quickly said choking back the tears. She went over and gave him a big hug. "How is my girl?" Daddy asked, "I'm good Daddy, really good" Leah told him. "Did you all have fun last night?" Leah felt really guilty not telling Daddy what had happened, but it wasn't just her secret to keep. All of the kids that was with them last night had snuck out and she couldn't tell. "Yeah Daddy, I had a great time last night" she finally said. "That's good" Daddy replied, "I'm going to need you to hurry and get dressed, there is a lot to do today, especially the big race down at the lake. We want to get there early to make sure that we have a good view of the race." "Yeah, the big race" Leah thought to herself, that's all they talked about last night, in fact that's how they ended up racing, practicing for the "big race."

It would have been O.K. with Leah if she had to miss the race. She wasn't sure how she would react seeing Mike again. She had kind of liked him in the beginning but now she just didn't. He was an airhead and a coward. He started backing down the minute that he saw Louie, not to mentioned the fact that he had tried to make the accident her fault and yelled at Sandy. She had lost all respect for him. She wasn't sure what she would say to him. They finished breakfast, cleaned up and got dressed for the race.

It was bitterly cold outside. The snowsuit helped but not a whole lot. Leah was very sore but she had to try not to show it. When they got to the lake some of the racers were already there. She had never seen anything like this before, people had started fires in trashcans away from the lake in an effort to try and keep warm. They were frantically rubbing their hands over the fire and drinking hot cider and cocoa. Leah and Sandy joined them. From the corner of her eye she could see Daddy watching her so she tried her best not to limp. She just stared at the lake, even though she had been there hours earlier she could not take her eyes away from its beauty. It was a little more than a mile across and appeared to be frozen solid, sort of a gray color. She just stood there staring as Daddy walked over to talk to her.

Her body was trembling, some from the cold and some from the fear. Daddy asked her again if she were enjoying herself and she said yes. He acted as if he knew that something was wrong but he didn't push the issue. Daddy took that opportunity to talk to Leah about her recent behavior, he didn't yell at her, he never did. He simply told her that he was not pleased with the way that things were going between her and Momma and that he wanted her to work harder to get along. He also let her know that she had to work harder at school and just to get herself together in general and stay out of trouble.

Leah looked over at Sandy who looked as if she were literally on pins and needles. She realized that Sandy was afraid that Daddy was finding out about last night so she quickly agreed to everything that Daddy had said and walked over to reassure Sandy. Then the rest of the racers started to show up. It would happen that Mike and Louie would show up just about the same time. Leah's heart was in her throat. She didn't know what to expect. Mike got off of his snowmobile and walked over to where the girls were standing. He asked Leah if she were O.K. and apologized to them again.

Leah wasn't listening to him anymore, over his shoulder she could see Louie heading toward them. She glanced around the lake to see where Daddy was so that she could run the other way if she had to. Daddy was talking and laughing with someone but it seemed that all of the teenagers with the exception of Mike and Sandy were watching Louie walk up behind Mike. Leah wanted to tell Mike to run but she was frozen with fear. As he got closer to the three of them, he reached out and put his hand on Mike's shoulder, "Is everything alright?" he asked the three of them. "Everything is fine Uncle Louie," Sandy assured him. "Good, then you probably want to get over to your machine and get ready for the race," Louie said to Mike in a threatening tone not taking his hand off of his shoulder and Mike was quick to take his advice. Louie hugged both girls and asked again if Leah was O.K. She told him that she was and he went off to prepare for the race.

Everybody was shocked to see Louie suited up for the race; it had been a few years since he had raced. He had decided not to compete in the big race about three years earlier after winning the race every year for six years in a row. No one could beat him and he had decided to bow out and give someone else a chance to win. This year was different, after what Mike had done Louie was determined not to let him win the race. He was the odds on favorite and had taken over Louie's reputation of being unbeatable. Louie couldn't beat him up physically so he had made a decision to take the race from him.

Mike was a true competitor, if Louie wanted the race he would have to take it from him. He was not about to roll over and just let him have it. The race was not marked by a trail; the only rule was that you had to go around the entire lake in order to win. No place was out of bounds. The unwritten rule was that you either rode the woods or the roads. At the end of the last bend was a five-foot drop from the road to the lake. It had always been that the first person to make it to the last bend would be the winner of the race. Today would prove to be a little different.

The race started, everyone in the race stayed close together until the second bend. That is when the leaders would establish themselves. Mike, Trevor, Uncle Harry, Louie's brother, and Louie would establish themselves as the leaders. Just like the night before the racers went into the woods, around trees, and on the road. The lead kept going back and forth with all of the racers concentrating on getting to the last bend first. They yelled at each other as the crowd cheered for their favorite racer. Trevor and Uncle Harry were leading the race, they kept challenging each other for position, going up hills and around trees before getting back on the road only to see that one or the other had gained a foot or two on the other.

Louie and Mike were not only fighting for second place it seemed to Leah that they were trying to kill each other. Their challenge for position was a lot more intense than the other guys. The other guys seemed to be having fun yelling and screaming but Louie and Mike were as serious as heart attacks. They were purposely trying to run each other off the road. It was as if no one was racing except for the two of them. Some people screamed, some held their breath, and some just stood there in horror. Everybody watched as turn after turn these guys tried to get into position to get to the last bend first.

Louie and Mike had spent so much time battling each other that they didn't realize how close they were to the end of the race, and Uncle Harry and Trevor were in front of them with less than two hundred yards until the last bend. That's when they both decided to make their moves. They powered through Uncle Harry and Trevor, Mike on the inside and Louie on the outside. Mike's inside position gave him an advantage as they approached the last bend but Louie would not be denied. Mike hit the bend a mega second before Louie but the position of the end of the trail would make it impossible for Louie to pass him. That is when Louie made his final move.

Instead of staying on the trail behind Mike, Louie went straight for the lake. Everyone screamed and Leah closed her eyes. It had been a long time since anyone had hit the lake during a race. They all knew that there was a chance that the lake wasn't frozen hard enough to withstand the force of the snowmobile hitting the ice at more than 70 mph. They knew it because as a younger man Louie had tried to do it on this same trail and ended up him and his machine had to be fished out of the lake with Louie suffering from hypothermia. That ordeal had cost him two of his toes even though they had gotten him out of the water pretty quickly.

Now here he was doing it again. Louie cleared the drop, it seemed as if were airborne forever. Everyone held their breath for what seemed like an eternity. Bam! Louie hit the ice, immediately everyone heard this loud cracking noise and saw the ice start to crack. Louie hit the accelerator, Whoom! His machine took off over the lake. Now he had the advantage, Mike could not believe his eyes. He nearly wrecked "his machine" trying to watch Louie. As Louie raced across the lake the ice continued to crack behind him. He barely made it to the other side of he lake before the ice started to break away.

Everyone started to scream, cheer and cry all at the same time. Leah could not believe what she had just seen. Louie came back up onto the trail and crossed the finish line well ahead of Mike who was so angry that he lost that he just kept riding. Uncle Harry and Trevor crossed the finish line as well as the other riders and they all jumped off their machines and came to jump all over and congratulate Louie who was himself ecstatic that he had made the jump and survived it this time. Leah just stood there glued to her spot. Daddy and Shari, Sandy and the rest of the family were all congratulating Louie, except for Grandma who was beating him with her hat and telling him to never do that again.

Louie looked up at Leah, "You ain't got no love for your Uncle?" he asked her as he stretched out his arms. Leah was still just standing there with both hands over her mouth, someone nudged her toward Louie and she have him the biggest hug ever. Daddy knew that something was going on. He had seen the exchange between the girls, Mike, and Louie before the race but he knew that Louie had everything under control. "The last one back to the cabin is a Girl," Louie shouted, which must be the ultimate insult in snowmobile language because even the girls scrambled to either get on their own machines, on with somebody or in any vehicle that would move in an effort not to be the last one back to the cabin.

The race was over and now everyone raced back to the "big house" where Auntie and some other family members had prepared a feast. Everyone in the community at least stopped by that day. All brought dishes to add to the feast that had already been prepared. They laughed and joked. Mostly about the look on Mike's face when Louie hit the lake. "It was as if he has been robbed at gunpoint" someone joked. Leah felt kind of sorry for him. All of his friends were at the party but he was nowhere in sight, not to mention the fact that winning was so important to him and he had just lost.

Louie went outside after a while, Leah just thought that he needed some air or was tired of all of the attention. He came back in after a few minutes and made his way over to where Leah was sitting. "You all right?" he asked her one last time. "Yeah, I'm O.K." Leah assured him. "Good, because there is somebody outside that wants to see you," he said as he walked away, "Holler if you need me."

Leah knew that it would be Mike out there waiting to talk to her. She went out and they talked for a while. Leah didn't want to be mean to him but she just didn't like him. Despite all that had gone on since she got to Daddy's house she still missed Jamie, really bad. She invited Mike in and lost herself in the crowd. She knew that she was going home tomorrow, and even though she had fun, had a new hero, and had met many new family members who seemed to really like her she missed home. She had to admit that she even missed her own family, even Momma. She wondered for a minute what they were doing, but whom she really missed was Jamie. She had to somehow make herself stop thinking about him. It only made her sad to think about him so she decided that just for now she wouldn't.

She got up and started to move around talking to people at the party. She spotted Mike off to the side looking as if he just wanted to disappear and went over to talk to him. He told her that he really liked her family, even how much he respected Louie. Mike's family was very well off but they did not spend much time together. Even in a place as small as Woodland Mike's parents had their own set of friends and for the most part that's where they spent their time. Leah felt lucky concerning her family for the first time that she could remember. She decided that she would go home and try to put her life back together. She decided that she did have some things to be thankful for. As the party ended she said good-bye to Mike who promised to see her at Christmas break, and went out to the cabin to pack her things. Things would be different from now on she thought. She had no idea how true that statement would turn out to be.

CHAPTER TEN

Thanksgiving 1995 had turned out to be very enlightening for Leah. Not only had she managed to have fun and make new friends, she had found her faith in mankind again. She had a brand new relationship with Daddy and Sheri, and had found a new friend in her stepsister Sandy. The most important lesson she felt that she had learned was how to be a teenager, how to go to school, make friends and have fun. She decided that she would give this new life a try.

She went back to school and got on top of her studies. The school spirit was high that year, there were three football games left in the season before the city and state champions would be crowned. It was a very exciting time for Leah. She had made a friend on the football team who was a distant cousin of one of her brothers. She was at every game and for the most part the drinking had slowed down drastically. She marched through the halls at school chanting school spirit songs and having a great time. She still missed Jamie a lot but she tried to stay focused on school so that she wouldn't think about him.

The last time that she had seen him was at her brother's house after Thanksgiving. Tammy wasn't there when she got there so she was able to give him a hug and talk to him for a while before she came. He told her that it was almost time for their baby to be born and that although he hadn't planned on it he was kind of looking forward to it. He was still in school, Leah knew that. Their schools had played against each other already and would do so again during the championships. Jamie had managed to stay in school and even excel. He was "all city" and "all state" that year. She couldn't help but to be proud of him. It was safe to say that she fell in love with him all over again that day. It didn't help matters much when he told her how much he missed her. The one statement that should have made her day brought her to tears, it hurt too much that they could not be together. Leah decided to leave before Tammy got there, she did not want to see them together and she sure didn't want to have to face the girl she had lost Jamie to, so she left.

Leah was determined not to think about them. She studied hard, and hung out with her new friends. She spent a lot of time at Daddy's house with Sandy and all of her new friends. She had a lot of fun during this time despite the ache in her heart that never seemed to go away. She was around kids her own age and doing age appropriate activities, she was hanging out with guys without having sex with them and it was good, but she stilled missed Jamie. It was impossible not to think about him, he was very popular around the high school circuit because of his football talents. The fact that he was very handsome didn't help matters much either.

She probably would have stood a chance to forget about him if not for the fact that their schools would meet for the city championships. For weeks over the Christmas holiday season she could think of little else but him. She had purposely stayed away from her brother's house in an effort not to run into him but it was inevitable. Brother was planning a New Years Eve party and Sandy wanted to go. Mostly she wanted Leah to go so that she would have a chance to see Jamie. Leah had been acting very brave but Sandy had caught her crying on several occasions and she knew that it was because she really missed Jamie.

There was another reason that Sandy wanted to see Jamie. Leah had hooked up with some new friends, friends that Sandy didn't like. These guys smoked a lot of weed and Sandy remembered very well what had happened the last time Leah had smoked weed. She also knew that there were very few people that Leah would listen to regarding this matter. She didn't want to tell her parents but she would if this didn't work. If Jamie couldn't convince Leah to stop hanging around this crowd she would have to tell.

Leah and Sandy were having a good time getting ready for the party. Leah took her time making sure that everything was perfect, her hair, clothes, and makeup had to be immaculate. It took her two hours to get ready with Sandy rushing her the whole time. They finally left for the party. When they got there it was already a full house. It was a good thing that Daddy and Sheri were dropping them off because there was nowhere to park. Sheri reminded them to be careful and have fun and they pulled off. They walked into the house and were greeted by Brother. Before he could even get a word out Leah heard Jamie's voice talking loud and laughing.

"No drama" she heard Brother say as Sandy grabbed her hand and they headed toward the voice. Leah immediately felt afraid. She knew that Brother's warning must mean that Tammy was there but Sandy didn't care. They continued to follow his voice and just about the time that Leah decided to try and slow down they turned the corner and ran right into him.

Jamie looked as if he had seen a ghost and it didn't take them long to figure out why as they looked over his shoulder and saw a very pregnant Tammy. Leah felt as if someone had knocked the wind out of her. Tammy had a strange look on her face that caught Leah's attention for a split second before she turned her gaze back to Jamie. "Hey" was all that he could manage to say to them. Sandy spoke to him but Leah couldn't even manage to say hey, she just stared at him for a minute petrified. He quickly turned around to look at Tammy and when he saw that she wasn't paying attention, he took Leah by the arm and guided her to another part of the house. It didn't seem that she would ever breathe again but she finally caught her breath. "Are you O.K?" he asked and asked again. She assured him that she was O.K. and before their conversation could go any further someone from behind them yelled "Hey Leah," and picked her up from behind.

It was Jamie's friend and teammate Toney. This time Leah managed to speak to their friend and tell him to put her down. He was genuinely happy to see her and gave her a big hug. Jamie just stood back and was kind of happy that Toney had come in at a very awkward moment. Leah seemed happy to see him too but Sandy was not so happy. She recognized Toney as one of the "new friends" that Leah had been hanging out with lately. She caught Jamie's eye from across the room and motioned for him to come over. As she began to tell him what was going on Jamie looked back over at his long time friend and his now x-girlfriend. He was not very happy at all.

Jamie hated drugs and everybody knew it. He knew that Toney smoked pot but he didn't know that he was trying to encourage Leah to smoke. Leah looked up just in time to see the anger in Jamie's eyes as he glared at first Toney and then her. He was just about to walk back across the room to confront them when Tammy touched his shoulder. As angry as he was at that moment it probably wouldn't have mattered except she was crying and holding her stomach. Jamie was torn for a moment but he had to see about Tammy because it was very close to her due date. He glared at her one last time before he put his arm around Tammy's shoulder and walked her over to the couch and sat down with her.

Leah had never seen that kind of anger on his face. She looked up at her sister with a "what did you say to him?" look on her face. Toney was clueless as to what was going on and was talking to someone else by now. Leah walked over to Sandy who immediately confessed what she had told him. "Why would you tell him that?" she remembered asking. It didn't matter; he looked up at her once more and then gave all of his attention to Tammy who was actually in labor. He knew that she wanted him to at least look at her but he didn't. She assumed that it was because he hated her now, but the truth was that if he looked at her now he would lose it and he had to concentrate on Tammy. So he left without even so much as a glance backwards.

Leah was devastated, and very angry with her sister. Sandy kept trying to apologize but Leah didn't want to hear it. She wanted to scream. Toney finally made it back over to where they were and even though he was as high as a kite he knew that Leah was hurting so he hugged her. "Come on and go hang out with us," he said in her ear. Sandy heard him and began to shake her head no, Leah had been doing so well and she didn't want her to get in trouble. Leah just looked at her blankly over Toney's shoulder. She was hurt worse than ever and there was only one way that she knew to ease the pain. So she took the drink out of Toney's hand, drank it, and asked him to get her coat. She just didn't want to feel anything so she left with Toney and his friends.

CHAPTER ELEVEN

Leah was in so much trouble with her Dad. He told her that she had to go back with her mother if she couldn't follow his rules. She was numb and didn't care. Tammy had her baby that night and Leah hadn't heard anything from Jamie since then. Toney told her that he couldn't hang out with her anymore, at least not until after the playoffs. He and Jamie had gotten into a fight and Jamie had threatened to tell the coach that not only was Toney getting high but that he was also getting young girls high as well. Leah was back drinking and now she was smoking pot as well. The only reason that she was going to school was so that she could meet up with her friends and get high.

There was plenty of excitement in the air. The state championship game was in less than two weeks. It would pit Leah and Jamie's schools against each other. The schools were archrivals and they both wanted to win badly. There was no education going on in those couple of weeks especially not for Leah who was high everyday now. It was a wonder that she didn't get into trouble but her mother just didn't seem to care No one did. It seemed that her Dad had gotten fed up with giving her chances and she really didn't blame him. She had to find out what was going on with Jamie so she called his Grandmother Fannie.

She begged Fannie to tell her what was going on and after warning her that she really didn't want to know she sat down with her the night before the big game and told her what Jamie had said. He was very angry and disappointed, he thought that Leah was smart, different from Tammy; he thought that she wanted something from life. Instead now he thought that she had turned out to be a stoner on her way to not graduating and turning out to be a nobody who hung out with losers. He thought that there was more than pot smoking going on between Leah and Toney and he was ticked of about it. Out of everything that Fannie said that night all that Leah heard was that he was jealous of her and Toney, that meant a lot to her so she got herself together and went to the game the next day.

The game wasn't even close. Jamie's team cleaned the floor with Leah's team. Jamie played corner back and as usual was brilliant scoring two touchdowns and would have scored three had Toney not missed a questionable block. When the game was over Toney was ready to hang out, he figured that Jamie couldn't get him in trouble, at least not this season because it was over. There would definitely be a party tonight for the team and he wanted Leah to come. Jamie was so mean to her that she thought this would be the ultimate way to get back at him so she went to the party. She figured that someone would tell him that she was there afterward but with the new baby, and his stand against drinking and smoking nobody, especially not Leah expected him to come to the party.

Leah had already taken a drink and was just standing around watching, and listening to the guys talk and laugh about the game. Some of the guys were trying to get Toney to admit that he had missed the block on purpose but he just laughed and denied it. As she looked at him at that moment she knew that he had missed the block on purpose. His eyes tried to convince her otherwise but she knew. She turned around and walked into the kitchen and poured another drink. Just as she was about to put it up to her mouth a hand reached around and took the drink from her. She knew that hand anywhere. She turned around and looked directly into Jamie's eyes.

"You don't need this," he said to her. She was embarrassed and hurt so she looked down. He lifted her head by the chin and repeated again that she didn't need the drink. "What are you doing here?" she asked him and before he could answer another voice said, "Yeah Sims, what are you doing here?" Jamie looked up at Toney who was very irritated that Jamie had decided to come to the party. He looked back at Leah and said, "This is a team party right, last I checked I was still a part of the team." "No man, what are you doing in here with my date, don't you have a wife and kid at home waiting for you?" he asked as he advanced toward Jamie. Leah stepped in between them as Jamie said, "You need to mind your business man."

"This is my business" Toney told him as he kept advancing. Jamie grabbed Leah's arm and gently pulled her out of the way.

This was crazy, Toney was twice Jamie's size and everyone thought that it would be no contest if it came down to it. At least those that didn't know

Jamie, if you knew him you knew that there was no quit in him. So Leah stepped between them again, "Jamie you should leave," she told him. "Sounds like good advice to me," Toney said. Jamie wasn't even a little scared; he looked at Leah and asked her to come with him. Toney tried to get her to stay, but she knew that if she stayed, Jamie would too so she left with him. She knew that Jamie would not back down and she also knew that Toney would probably hurt him really bad.

The only place that they had to go was to Fannie and Brother's house so that is where they went. Fannie was ecstatic to see them together so of course she let them stay together. And that is exactly what they did. They spent the night together comforting each other. Reassuring each other how much in love they still were despite everything that had gone on. They needed to be together tonight no matter what happened tomorrow. They were irresponsible and careless and it didn't matter, at least not tonight. It would only begin to matter about six weeks later when Leah realized that she hadn't gotten her period.

CHAPTER TWELVE

Things had come full circle for Leah and Jamie. Once again they were sneaking around behind Tammy's back seeing each other. The only thing that was different was that now Leah didn't insist that Jamie tell Tammy they were seeing each other. She knew that this meant they would not be able to be together anymore and nothing in her mind was worth that. Leah did everything in her power to prove to Jamie that she was the girl that he thought she was. She focused on school and did whatever else he asked her to, including not hanging around Toney anymore.

Her life had turned back into that roller coaster ride, one minute she was with Jamie laughing and enjoying each other's company and the next she was watching him with Tammy. It was a really hard time for Jamie and Tammy also. Tammy did not know how to take care of a baby and more and more it had become evident that she did not have the desire to learn. Little Jamie was back and forth in the hospital in those first couple of months with colds and flu and finally ended up there with pneumonia. It became very evident to Leah that no matter what Jamie was telling her during those precious moments, he really did love Tammy because despite all the mistakes that she was making, he kept taking her back.

That clarity had come just a little bit too late though. On Valentine's Day Leah had waited for Jamie all day long. She knew and had accepted that he would spend part of the day with Tammy but she had at least expected to see him. Instead Jamie had called that evening to say that he would not be able to get away to see her. She, for the first time did not let him know how devastated she was, something in her just would not allow her to be sad that day. Instead, she got angry, hung up the phone and would not accept or return his calls. She thought about it all night long. She was really tired of playing second fiddle to his real life knowing full well that things were not going to change. She made in her mind that something had to change but she wasn't sure how to change things.

She began to go over in her mind how she could confront him once again and force him to decide who he really wanted to be with. Even if he decided that he wanted to be with Tammy, at least she wouldn't feel so stupid sitting around waiting for him. Maybe she should make him jealous by calling Toney again. Except for the fact that Toney wasn't speaking to her anymore and had even told her that the only reason that he had asked her out in the first place was to make Jamie mad. He later apologized and admitted he was just angry with her, but he made it perfectly clear that he didn't want to go out with her anymore. She had to find a way off of this roller coaster.

Unfortunately, fate would decide that ride would have to last a little longer and hurt a lot more before it was over. Leah finally talked to Jamie the next day and told him that she just didn't want to go through this thing with him anymore. This was the first time that Leah had spoken to him the way she had. She was genuinely fed up with the situation and she wanted out. Jamie had no choice but to accept what she said. She even thought that he was a little relieved that she had come to this conclusion. She had no idea how much it would hurt not to see him, how much she would actually miss him, but she was determined to stay away.

The pain and loneliness was a lot more than Leah could take. It had been a while since she had felt pain like this and she just didn't want to feel this. Nothing was right anymore, there was no hope for her and Jamie, and she was just plain tired of trying. Trying to be good, trying to go to school, trying to stay out of trouble, and most of all trying not to drink or smoke pot. She thought that things would be so much easier for her if she could just laugh, if she could just not think about her situation for a little while. She was ready to give up on everything school, home, and Jamie. So she pretended to go to school but instead she went and found some of Toney's friends and got high. For the next few weeks she didn't give herself a chance to sober up long enough to feel anything. She was determined not to call Jamie even though he had told her to call if she changed her mind. But everyday that he didn't call her hurt more so she continued on her binge. She wasn't paying any attention to the fact that she was feeling sick every morning. She had chalked it up to having had too much to drink.

She never thought that it could be anything different until she decided that her binge had gone on long enough. For the first few days in March she had stopped drinking and smoking. It wasn't until a few days later that she realized that the morning nausea had not stopped. This particular morning it was as bad as it had ever been. Usually she could grab some toast or crackers and it would go away but not this morning. Leah hurried to make the toast and eggs knowing that Momma was watching her. It must have been written all over her face.

She ate the toast and eggs and for a brief moment was relieved. Momma was still watching out of the corner of her eye, so when the nausea came back moments later Leah tried to hurry and leave for school, but she never made it to the door. She vomited all over the hallway floor. She instantly knew what the problem was and so did Momma. " I guess you satisfied now" was the sarcastic remark that came. Leah was terrified, 'Oh My God', what was she going to do now? She had never felt so afraid in her life. As she cleaned up the mess she began to wonder how in the world she was going to tell Jamie, he would be so mad.

And what had she done to this baby? She had been getting high for weeks now and Jamie knew it. He was going to kill her. She didn't know how he was going to find out but she made up her mind that she was not going to be the one to tell him, and she didn't want to be anywhere around when he found out.

Momma continued to ridicule her. "Didn't that boy just have a baby, how is he going to take care of two babies without a job?" Momma went on talking until Leah was done cleaning up the mess saying every negative thing that came to her mind, "Just because you are having that boy's baby does not mean he is going to be with you" she said. Leah got so angry when she heard these words, "He's going to know that you are trying to trap him into something," she went on to say. These were the meanest, cruelest things Leah had ever heard Momma say, and she had been cruel to her most of her life.

What would she do if Jamie felt this way? "He wouldn't, would he?" she asked herself. When Leah left out of the door for school Momma was still talking, "You gone end up raising that baby by yourself, don't expect no help from me." Was the last thing she heard her mother say before she closed the door.

The cold March air began to clear her mind, it was also starting to help with the nausea. "Momma was so cruel," she thought to herself, "Jamie would never act that way," she found herself saying out loud. He was one of the good guys; he didn't treat girls that way. He was helping Tammy take care of her baby even though he didn't want to. He had stepped up and become a father to Little Jamie and he would do the same for their child. "Wouldn't he?" she asked herself. Of course he would. If this was true then what was the lump in her throat about, why this uneasy feeling in the pit of her stomach? It wouldn't be long before she had the answers to all of her questions.

Leah couldn't bring herself to get on the bus that would take her to school. Instead, she waited for the next bus that would take her to Fannie's house. She knocked and knocked but no one came to the door. Fannie and Brother had recently broken up and she didn't want anything to do with Brother or his family. Leah knocked again; still no one came to the door. It was early in the morning so Leah convinced herself that maybe Fannie was still sleeping even though she knew that she wasn't. She knew that Fannie was just tired of all of the drama and didn't want to be a part of it anymore.

It was so cold outside, Leah didn't have any more money to go anyplace else and even if she had money, where would she go? If she went back home Momma would pick up where she left off, she really didn't think that she could fit in at school now, Daddy and Sheri were at work so she couldn't go there. Leah just sat on the porch and began to cry. Something down deep told her that this is what she had to look forward to. She felt abandoned; she thought Fannie was her friend. This changed everything in her life. She would just walk to Daddy's and stay outside somewhere until they came home.

Just then she heard someone at Fannie's door. Fannie had looked outside and saw her crying. No matter what was going on with her and Brother she couldn't let Leah stay outside in the cold. She let her in and gave her something to drink, Fannie knew better than anyone how much Leah loved Jamie. She had tried to help them on so many occasions but things had just not worked out. She felt sorry for Leah but she was going to tell her that she could no longer be in the middle. Jamie and Tammy had been there together a few days earlier vowing to make things work out and Fannie had made a promise to herself not to interfere anymore. She realized that she had been deep in thought and that it was time to talk to Leah.

As she sat down to talk to her she noticed that she was still crying, she thought that maybe she had talked to Jamie on the phone and found out his plan, but no, Jamie had told Fannie that Leah had broken up with him. What was wrong with this child and why was she involving her once again? She watched her continence for a few moments and realized that something was terribly wrong. She had never seen this kind of sadness before in Leah. She gave her some tissue and asked her what the problem was. Leah tried to tell her but it wouldn't come out past the sobs. The things that Momma had said kept ringing in her head and she could not stop herself from crying.

Fannie didn't know what was wrong but she had known enough of her own pain to know that this child needed to be comforted. Leah slid down on her knees and began to openly sob, uncontrollably. Fannie slid down to her knees with her and asked again what was wrong. Leah still couldn't answer her so Fannie reached out put her arms around her and began to rock her and tell her that everything would be O.K. Leah began to shake her head no trying to tell Fannie that nothing would ever be O.K. again. She had really messed up this time; everyone would abandon her now even Fannie as soon as she found out what she had done. She felt so stupid and alone.

Leah cried until she was empty, she was weak and had no more tears or energy to shed them. She sat there on the floor for a few minutes longer until she collected herself and began to tell Fannie what the problem was. She told Fannie everything that Momma had said to her that morning. Fannie became upset herself; this child had been through enough with this crazy family of hers. One thing was for sure, she was not going to give up on her and she would not allow her Grandson to either. He helped to make this baby no matter what the circumstances were and she was going to make sure that he helped to take care of it. She spoke these words to Leah and she began to feel better, what she didn't realize was that Fannie could make Jamie take care of the baby but, she couldn't make him choose Leah over Tammy and she would soon find that out.

CHAPTER THIRTEEN

Jamie was furious when he found out about the baby. All of the things that Momma had said to her, he said that and more. Fannie had told her to expect that from him and to give him a chance to calm down after she told him. Because of the warning Leah was not completely devastated by what Jamie said. She was hurt true enough, but she realized that some of things that Jamie said were being spoken out of anger and hurt. Jamie felt tricked and betrayed by Leah. She of all people knew what he was facing; all of the problems with Tammy and the baby were getting to him.

Tammy had decided that she didn't want to be a teenaged Mom; so much of the burden of raising Little Jamie had fallen on Jamie. He was devastated that she would not only treat him the way that she was treating him, but to abandon their child was much more than Jamie could understand. He was frustrated and disillusioned; the last thing that he needed to hear was that Leah was pregnant. He told her that he would take care of the baby financially, but that he would never have anything else to do with her.

One thing was for sure as far as Leah was concerned. She was having a baby and now that everyone knew about it, it gave her great pleasure to hold on to her stomach in expectation. Unlike Momma and Jamie this baby would not give it's love and then take it back when times got rough. This baby would love her unconditionally and she was looking forward to that kind of love for a change.

It didn't matter that Momma was upset, Daddy was disappointed, or that Jamie hated her right now. The only thing that mattered to her was that the baby would be O.K. She was concerned because she had spent the first months of her pregnancy drinking and smoking. She had to get to the doctor and make sure that the baby was healthy. She had to take care of it. She had to show the baby the kind of love that she had never been shown. She couldn't wait to hold it in her arms and to rub it's little nose with her own.

She wanted to snuggle its little neck and inhale deeply, to smell the scent of the baby that she would love without ceasing. No matter how anybody else felt, this was a bond that could not be broken.

Momma would give Leah such a hard time that she would move in with Fannie. Brother was out of her life and her mother had recently passed away so she was happy for the company. She was also angry with Jamie for the way that he was treating Leah so she decided that she would help out as much as she could. Leah enrolled in night school and did everything that she could to change Jamie's mind but he had made a decision to stay with Tammy. It was a painful situation but Leah was determined to be strong for her and her baby.

One thing that she didn't realize was that her decision to move in with Fannie meant that she was desperately trying to hold on to a dead situation. There was really no future for her and Jamie but she refused to believe it. Every now and then Jamie would show up and spend a minimal amount of time with Leah and because she was so naive and truly believed that they would end up together, she settled for the little time that she could get with him.

The further that she got along in her pregnancy the less she saw of Jamie. It was getting harder and harder to stay around his family and she realized that the time had come when she had to let go of him and move on. Her sister Jeanne had gotten married and moved into her new home. It really was not a good environment for Leah and the baby due to the ongoing party atmosphere but she had to get away from Jamie and his family. She decided against Fannie's advice to move in with her sister and her new husband.

Leah spent the summer months wishing that the baby would come early. As the time drew near she became more and more restless. The doctor had told her that the baby was fine and she just wanted to hold it and love it. The baby stayed right on schedule though. Leah had started to feel better about herself now that she wasn't pining away waiting for Jamie to pay her the least bit of attention. She still missed him but she had faced the fact that he didn't want to be with her. Now she just wanted to go on with her life but everything was on hold until she had the baby.

She couldn't go back to school in September because she was too far along in her pregnancy. Nor could she get a job, or meet someone new. She was staying with Jeanne but she was miserable. They partied all the time but the thing that Leah hated the most was the way Jeanne disciplined her children. She hated hearing them cry and she and Jeanne would often argue about the way that she treated her niece and nephew. The end result of the fights would always be that she would be even angrier with the kids and treat them worse.

Leah didn't know what to do. She couldn't stay and not say anything about the way that Jeanne was treating the kids, and she knew that if she said anything that would make her sister even angrier, so for the most part she tried to keep the kids under her sister's radar so they wouldn't get into trouble. Even that after a while stopped working, Jeanne started to feel as if Leah was telling her how to raise her kids and she would look for reasons to spank the kids. Leah knew that this was not the place for her. Now she began to ask God was there any place for her. Was there a place that she and her baby could be safe? She just wanted it long enough for her baby to be born and she could finally settle someplace of her own.

She was just turning sixteen but she felt like an old woman most of the time. Her friends and sisters were out having fun. Her sister Ina had had a baby but she and Lynn continued to have fun and party as if nothing was wrong. She knew that they had gone through pretty much the same things as she had and yet it didn't seem to faze them a bit. She didn't understand why everything bothered her so much, why she never felt comfortable in her own skin. She didn't understand this continuous urge to run every time things did not go her way. She didn't understand it, but she knew she couldn't stay with Jeanne and her husband. She just had to figure out where she was going. She didn't know that as she was thinking a temporary solution was on the way.

Jeanne and her husband were planning a party. Leah was desperate to have this baby now. She remembered that Ina had gone into labor after riding a bike to the store so she thought that if she did something really strenuous it make her labor come sooner. She cleaned the house from top to bottom, mopping the floors and moving furniture around. She ran up and down the stairs waiting on people hand and foot. She was so tired by the end of the party that she just crashed, but no labor.

She woke up the next day disappointed that she had not gone into labor. She moped around all day talking to the baby and trying to encourage it to come out. Late in the afternoon she decided to get up and start picking up after the party. Jeanne and her husband stayed in their room for most of the day and the kids were hiding out in their room. She gathered all the cups and plates and threw them away; she also threw away all the bottles and put all the cans in a separate bag to take back to the store.

One of the cans missed the bag and rolled over up under the table, Leah bent over reached and get the can to put back in the bag. When she began to straighten up she felt the most incredible pain underneath her stomach. It caused her to stay bent for about fifteen seconds before she could stand completely straight. "WOW!," she had never felt anything like that before so she just stood there for a minute. Nothing happened so she continued to clean up what was left from the party. When she was done she sat down to watch T.V. and another of those pains hit her. This time she screamed and her sister and brother-in-law came to see what was wrong. Leah had gotten her wish she was in labor

CHAPTER FOURTEEN

The labor was long and hard but worth every minute to Leah. God had given her a beautiful baby girl whom she had decided to name Bianca. She was a beautiful, golden brown baby with her father's dark eyes and her mother's face. She was by far the most beautiful baby that Leah had ever seen and she looked so much like her father that it was amazing. Too bad they had been in the hospital for two days and he had not even bothered to show up to see her. Leah was confused, didn't he even want to see what his beautiful daughter looked like, how could he just not show up? Out of all the times she had allowed Jamie to hurt her this one was different.

This time when the pain became too much to bear she got out of bed and went to the nursery. She took one look at her beautiful baby girl and her heart began to melt. She picked her up out of the crib and began to snuggle with her, rubbing her nose across Bianca's little face. The baby responded with little coos and all of a sudden the pain began to dissipate. She took a deep breath and realized that whatever happened, she would love this baby and the baby would love her back. This was a brand new feeling for Leah. It was as if for the first time since she could remember, she could take a deep breath. Things were not the way that she wanted them, not in the least but she somehow had the courage to face whatever life had for her and her baby.

Momma had showed up at the hospital and fell in love with the baby. It was a way of mending fences for the two of them. Momma said Leah and the baby could move back home as long as Leah went back to finish school. The day they were to be discharged Jamie finally showed up. He had bought a few things for the baby, but was still chasing after Tammy who by now did not want him. Leah took a good look at Jamie that day. Something was different, she didn't feel light headed, or like melting in his presence. In fact she felt sort of indifferent towards him.

How dare he show up three days after his baby was born. How dare he stand there beaming with pride after the way he had treated them. She knew that she was done chasing him, she didn't know how or when it had happened but she knew that her feelings had changed drastically for Jamie. Everything was changing. She felt as if she were in a whirlwind not sure where she was going to be when she landed.

She went home with Momma and after few weeks started going back to school. She appreciated being back at home but it wasn't long before she started to feel uncomfortable there as well. Momma was trying to take over the baby or so Leah thought. One thing was for sure, Leah thought that Momma had done such a poor job of raising her that there was no way she would allow her to raise her daughter. She called her sister Anna who by now had joined the Air Force along side her husband. She told Leah that she needed some temporary help with the kids and asked her to come to Ohio.

Leah decided to go. She was tired of everything and everybody in Detroit. Momma was fussing and she couldn't even find Jamie to tell him. She left a message for him with Fannie. Out of all the people in Detroit she would miss Fannie, she had truly been a friend to her. But it was time to go and she couldn't let anything or anybody stop her. She knew that she would be back but for now it was time to see what life had to offer her once she was free from all of the demons that haunted her in Detroit. Anna paid for the ticket and once again Leah was on the bus headed for Ohio, but this time she had her beautiful baby girl with her. She looked out of the window as the bus pulled out of the station, Good Bye Detroit! Leah was on her way to a new beginning, she just didn't know to the beginning of what.

Book Two

CHAPTER FIFTEEN

Leah and Bianca settled into their life in Ohio pretty quickly. Anna had just had another baby as well and was just getting back to her position in the Air Force. Leah would stay home and get her nephews and nieces off to school in the morning and then cook and clean and watch her niece Ne-Ne along with Bianca. This was her daily routine and she took pride in helping to take care of her sister's family. Anna was so much different than Jeanne. Leah knew that Jeanne loved her kids but she didn't know how to show it. Anna on the other hand was kind and gentle. She always had been.

There was only one problem with the arrangement that they had made. Leah had no income so she had to depend on Anna and her husband to take care of her and the baby. Jamie had the nerve to be angry that they had left Detroit and was not helping support the baby, and because she was taking care of the kids she didn't go out and look for a job. She hadn't learned to support herself. Momma had long since stopped working and just started to collect welfare. This had been all that she knew for a long time and she couldn't do that because Momma was still collecting welfare for her and now for the baby.

Anna and Gary were good to her and the baby. They did as much as could be expected of them to help take care of them financially. Still Leah didn't want to be a burden on them, she knew how to do hair so she would braid her nieces and the neighborhood young girls hair for a few dollars here and there. This was only a temporary situation she told herself so this would have to work for now. And it was working out just fine. Anna truly appreciated the help Leah gave her with the kids and Leah truly appreciated being in a quiet "normal" environment. It wouldn't be long before her image of the perfect suburban life would be shattered.

For the most part the daily life of Leah and the baby was good. She had met friends her age and was starting to hang out and get to know them. Two friends in particular were the twins Sheila and Michelle. She was friendly with Sheila but Michelle was her dearest and closest friend. They were all a few years older than Leah but no one knew except Michelle. Michelle's boyfriend Rickey was not only very popular but he was a very kind young man. He had plenty of friends and always an invitation to go someplace. Leah loved hanging out with them the only thing was no one in that circle was interested in her.

That didn't matter much to Leah though. She had a beautiful baby girl who was the center of her world. When she looked at Bianca she saw nothing but love looking back at her. Bianca was the one thing in Leah's life that seemed to be right. Leah wasn't in school so she got to spend her days loving her and watching her grow. Ne-Ne was also a beautiful baby girl. They would spend hours in the park with people just plain marveling over how beautiful the girls were.

The girls were growing up very quickly and they were a handful. It was starting to get harder to keep up with them. Anna and Gary had an extremely large unit and it was definitely the girls' territory. They ran and played all over the place. Leah hated to have them in the playpen all day so she would let them play all through the house as she went about her daily routine. They both had their way of commanding Leah's attention. They would do what most babies do and just start crying. Leah would have to stop her daily chores and comfort first one then the other.

Leah realized that these girls had her number. By now they were crawling all over the place and were impossible to keep up with. She decided that she had to keep them in the playpen while she did her chores but they had a different plan. Both of them would scream and cry until Leah would relent and take them out of the playpen, comfort them and allow them to roam freely. Leah decided that the sooner that she got her chores done the sooner she would be able to sit back and watch the girls play. This was her new plan.

This was a particularly beautiful late spring morning. Michelle had already called and said she wanted to go down to the tennis courts again today. She and Leah had begun this new diet and exercise regimen, which by the way had been working tremendously well. They both looked good, Leah looked better than she ever had in her life. She wanted to hurry and finish all of her chores so that she could dress herself and the girls and get to the tennis courts with Michelle.

She turned the T.V. on for the girls; there was a new show about a purple dinosaur that the girls loved. That always kept their attention. She started in the kitchen with the breakfast dishes. She went about her daily routine in record time and then moved to the dining area. The unit was very spacious and was made up like a big square. Coming into the front door the first thing you would see would be the staircase directly in front of you that led to the second floor bedrooms and bath room which was at the top of the stairs. To the right would be the living room area and directly behind the living room was the dining area, to the left was the kitchen, straight through the kitchen was the laundry room, to the left of the laundry room was the den and a left in the den would take you past the bathroom and put you back at the front door, which she would open to let the unit air out.

This is the routine that she followed to clean the house. Everything was child proofed so she wasn't worried about the girls as she moved with lightening speed through her chores. She cleaned every nook and cranny as she did everyday and finally made it around to the den. It took her only a second to notice that Bianca was the only one sitting in the middle of the floor watching T.V. and playing with the toys.

She instantly had a flashback of the girls getting stuck in the small downstairs bathroom by going into the bathroom, closing the door, and opening the drawers on the console that were immediately behind the door so that they blocked anyone from coming into the bathroom. Couple that with the fact that neither of them had the good sense to close the door and you get the hour-long fiasco that had occurred a couple of weeks earlier. Leah and Anna trying to get the girls to close the drawers so that they could get them out of the bathroom, and the girls standing there crying wanting to get out. Eventually, Bianca had the sense to finally stop crying long enough to close the drawer so that the girls could get out of the bathroom.

She went straight to the bathroom but Ne-Ne was not in the there. She went straight to the front door, the screen door was closed but it wasn't locked so she stepped outside and looked up and down the street. The street was quiet and there was no sign of Ne-Ne. Leah's heart began to race. She ran back into the house and checked every inch of the downstairs. She looked in every room, behind every piece of furniture and still no Ne-Ne. She picked up the phone to call the police and decided to call her brother-in-law instead. He was such a prankster, Leah just wanted to make sure that he hadn't come in while she was distracted with her chores and taken the baby to scare her.

The minute that he answered the phone at his office she panicked, she knew that this meant that the baby was really missing. Gary heard the panic in her voice and yelled at her to tell him what the problem was. "I can't find Ne-Ne," she cried to him. "What do you mean you can't find her?" he asked her. She went on to explain to him how she put the girls down to play while she cleaned up and came back to find only one of the girls. He told her to call the Air Force Police and that he was on his way.

Leah hung up the phone and called the police, she gave them all of the information while she looked through the house again. The police said that they were on their way; Leah continued to look through the house. She placed Bianca in the playpen so that she wouldn't get away while she continued to look for her niece. "It was impossible for her to be gone!" Leah thought but the more she looked for the baby the more convinced she became that she was gone. She must have wondered outside while she was vacuuming and someone must have taken her. Leah ran back outside frantically calling her niece's name. The neighbors started to come out and when she told them what was going on they said they had not seen the baby but began to help her look.

Leah was in a full-scale panic by the time the police got there. They were trying to calm her down and find out exactly what happened. They were asking the stupidest questions she thought at the time. "What was she wearing, how old was she, what did she look like?" She didn't want to answer any questions; she just wanted to find the baby. She was hysterical, "She's wearing a purple outfit, she eleven months old and has long curly hair and beautiful brown eyes," she said through the tears. There were several police cars by now. They were questioning neighbors and searching the area.

The officer that Leah was talking to led her back to Gary and Anna's unit. As they approached the unit she heard the officer say "OH MY GOD." She looked up just as the officer ran into the unit; he headed straight for the stairs just inside the unit and took them two at a time. When he got to the top he stood there for a second looking down at the floor. Leah followed his gaze down to the lifeless body of her niece. She closed her eyes and began to scream. Just then Gary came up behind her and started to shake her, "What. What?" he kept asking her.

Leah opened up her eyes and pointed up the stairs. Gary saw the officer bent over his baby and gasped. "Oh My God," he whispered as he headed for the door with Leah right behind him. The officer was bent over Ne-Ne with his face close to hers listening. "How did she get up there?" Leah asked out loud to no one in particular. Leah was thinking now "Who could have taken her up those stairs, she hadn't heard anything. There were fifteen steep stairs and the girls were afraid to go up the stairs, how did she get up there?"

A chuckle from the officer and a sigh of relief from her brother-in-law brought her back to reality. Leah looked up the stairs and saw the officer picking Ne-Ne up. Just then Ne—Ne whipped her eye and Leah stopped breathing for what seemed like an eternity. Ne-Ne started to whine and reach for her Daddy, all of the people standing around had her scared. Gary brought her downstairs; his tears had turned into a big wide grin. When he got to the bottom of the stairs Ne-Ne reached for Leah. She grabbed her and walked to a corner in the living room holding on to her so tight that the baby squirmed.

"Guess who learned how to climb the stairs today?" she heard the officer joke but she was in another world by then. She was examining the baby to make sure that everything was O.K. and she was kissing and hugging her at the same time. All was well, evidently, while Leah was vacuuming Ne-Ne had decided to challenge the stairs and she won. Unfortunately, or perhaps fortunately when she got to the top of the stairs she must have been really tired and so she had lain there and went to sleep.

It was a good thing that she had, what would have happened if she had tried to come back down the stairs? It scared Leah to think about it. It was a good thing that she didn't have to, she looked over at Bianca in the playpen sleeping. Ne-Ne was falling asleep in her lap, of course they were sleep it was their naptime, so she reluctantly laid the baby in the playpen next to hers. Her routine would have to change; the girls would have to stay in the playpen while she cleaned. They were getting into too much stuff and she couldn't take the chance of anything happening to them. She started to cry, her brother-in-law and the officer came over to console her, everything would be all right.

CHAPTER SIXTEEN

Leah had to bite the bullet and learn to let the girls cry while she did her chores. Most days they just cried themselves to sleep. Leah had learned to enjoy her afternoons at the tennis courts and the exercise was paying off tremendously. Her routine of getting the house clean while the girls played, and the dinner ready while the girls napped was great. After the girls nap they would all walk over to the tennis courts and play for a couple of hours. The girls loved being outside and Leah loved the exercise. "Wow," Michelle's Uncle Ernie had said to them one day, "These brothers had better look out, you ladies are looking good."

Leah felt like she looked good for the first time in her life. Lots of guys were trying to talk to her lately, but she had not been interested in any of them. She was having far too much fun and she just had not met anyone who caught her eye. Uncle Ernie was a sweet heart, he was doing pretty much the same thing for Michelle that Anna and Gary was doing for Leah. He had brought Michelle up from Florida to take care of his kids while he and his wife worked. Uncle Ernie was in the Air Force and his wife was a civilian secretary. She was the first person Leah had met since she stopped going to church that claimed to love the Lord.

Uncle Ernie and Cindy had a great family. Cindy had a young daughter named Sara from a previous marriage and they had a son together, little Ernie. Sara had Sickle Cell Anemia and was sick a lot. Ernie loved this little girl so much that it was hard to tell that she wasn't his. Leah respected him so much. They had come to be great friends despite the fact that Leah knew that Uncle Ernie had a secret life. She and Michelle both knew the secret but it somehow didn't take away from the respect that she had for him. She had made a conscious decision to keep the secret because people that she loved could be hurt if she told. Besides it was all in fun.

Leah had found out about the secret by accident. Anna loved to play Bingo and so on Tuesdays they would go to the Bingo hall. Anna had even gotten a job there after a while. One particular Tuesday Leah walked into Anna's room while she was getting ready for Bingo. She saw Anna putting rollers in hair rollers in her purse. She didn't pay any attention; Anna often would roll her hair in the car on the way home from Bingo. "Listen, I'll just be dropping you off at Bingo tonight with Lois," Anna told her, "I'll be back by the time Bingo is over."

"Where are you going?" Leah asked her. "Don't worry about that and you can't tell Gary that I didn't stay for Bingo." Anna told her. "Do you understand?" Leah didn't, but she said she did, she had been quite lucky at Bingo lately and she wanted to go.

The three of them left for the Bingo Hall. Lois and Anna were busy giggling about whatever it was that she was about to do. Leah didn't understand but it was O.K., Anna seemed to be having fun. When they got to the Bingo Hall, Anna let Leah and Lois off in front. She promised to be back by the time Bingo was over, Leah went into the Bingo Hall but Lois stayed back to talk to Anna. She walked into the hall and realized that she had left her purse in the car.

She turned around and started back outside, passing Lois on the way in, "I forgot to get my purse," she said as she ran past her. She stepped outside and looked around, she saw Anna's car going through the parking lot. There was another familiar car right behind her. Anna pulled into a parking space and Leah took a step toward the parking lot. The familiar car stopped right behind Anna; she got out of her car and got into the car with, who was this? Leah knew this car but she couldn't remember who it was. They drove right by her on the way out of the parking lot.

It was Uncle Ernie! "Oh My God!" she heard herself say. Lois was behind her telling her that she would give her the money to play but Leah was stuck. She was just standing there in disbelief. She thought that Anna and Gary were happy; she thought that Ernie and Cindy were happy. She couldn't believe what she had just seen. Lois was pulling Anna into the hall. "Girl come on, it's not the end of the world." No it wasn't the end of the world, but it was the end of what Leah believed about being happily married, "No one was happily married," she thought, "If Anna and Ernie weren't happily married, no one was, there was just no such thing."

Leah was being taught lesson after lesson regarding the way things really were. Her idealistic ways of thinking were being shattered time after time.

She was back to not knowing what to believe anymore. She had to keep moving forward though and it appeared to her that she was just going through the motions now. She still got up every morning and went through her daily routine of cleaning and cooking so that she could meet Michelle for their afternoon exercise routine. They had to exercise indoors now because of the cold weather but she was looking forward to it.

In fact she was doing just that a few days after she had found out about Anna and Uncle Ernie. She had been lost in her own thoughts when she heard her baby cry. The cry shook her out of her thoughts and she realized that Bianca must have been crying for a long time. For a brief moment Leah considered going into the other room and picking the baby up. She reasoned with herself that if she did it would slow down her process, Bianca would probably try to convince her to let her out of the playpen and Leah had learned her lesson in that area.

She reasoned with herself further that Bianca was dry and fed and there was no real reason for her to be crying. Leah kept right on doing what she was doing. "She'll cry herself to sleep," Leah said out loud as she continued cleaning. Leah became lost in her own thoughts once again as she went back to going through the motions of cleaning the house. A few minutes later she realized that Bianca had stopped crying. She was very pleased with herself for having not given in to the baby's cry.

Something about the quiet did not feel quite right. This quiet gave Leah an uneasy feeling. She peeked around the corner to take a look at the girls. Both of them were still in the playpen, both of them were quiet and appeared to be sleeping. Something deep inside urged Leah closer to the girls that day. The first face that she saw was Ne-Ne's; she was sleeping so peacefully that it almost seemed that she had a smile on her face. Leah could not help but smile as she remembered the recent drama that this beautiful baby had caused.

Then she turned her attention toward her own baby who also appeared to be sleeping peacefully. Instantly she knew that something was not right with the baby's color, a closer look showed her that there was partially dried blood coming from Bianca's nose. She moved next to the playpen and leaned closer to Bianca, she was not moving at all, nor was she breathing. "Oh My God!," Leah screamed, she snatched Bianca from the playpen and started to shake her as she called out her name. "Bianca! Bianca!" she kept saying, but the baby was as limp as a dishrag.

She put the baby on the floor and began to blow small breaths into her mouth. "Come on Bianca, please breathe," she kept saying between breaths. This went on for what seemed like an eternity to Leah, she was crying and pleading for her baby to breathe but nothing was happening. "God please help me!," she called out, she breathed a few more breaths into her daughter's mouth, out of frustration she let out an ear piercing scream waking up Ne-Ne who immediately began to cry. Just as she was about to give up, Bianca started to cough. It was a weak cough, but a cough just the same.

A blanket of hope covered Leah as she continued to breathe for her baby. She cleaned the nearly dried blood from Bianca's nose and face. Now Bianca was gasping for air, she was breathing but it was very hard for her to catch her breath. Leah ran to the phone to call an ambulance. They were only down the street so they were there in minutes and Leah and the baby were on their way to the hospital. She called Michelle before she left, told her what had happened, and asked her to get Ne-Ne from the neighbor.

The paramedics were giving Bianca oxygen, which was hard because she was scared and crying. It was still very hard for her to breathe and even harder for them to figure out why. They could see the dried blood in her nostrils and had assumed that she had just simply had a nosebleed. They continued to work on her until they got her to the hospital. The doctors were waiting for them. The paramedics started rattling off vital signs as they rushed Bianca in the back. Leah was crying again, she didn't know what to think, they were still working on Bianca and now they were telling her that she couldn't go back with them.

Her cries were coming in sobs now. She could not believe what was happening, she could not believe that God would take away the one person that she loved the most. Leah had not prayed in a long time but she did know how to, but the only words that she could think to say to God at that moment was, "God, please don't take my baby, I'll do whatever you want but please, just don't take my baby."

Anna was there by now, she was shaking Leah and asking her what happened. "I don't know, I don't know," Leah screamed at her. The nurse came out and started to ask Leah questions. She didn't want to answer any questions; she wanted someone to answer her questions. Leah sat down and put her arms over her head. Anna started to answer the lady's questions about Bianca. Gary was there by now and so was Uncle Ernie. Leah couldn't begin to think about any one else except her baby.

Gary came and put his arms around Leah, when she looked up at his face she became even more frightened, he never cried in front of people and now even he was crying. He tried to tell her that everything was going to be O.K., so did Uncle Ernie, it seemed as if all the guys from Gary's office were in and out of the emergency room while they waited. Most of them she knew or had heard of. One in particular, Sgt. Windsor was a good friend of Gary and Uncle Ernie. Leah had never met him but she had heard a lot about him. He was there showing a great deal of concern.

Leah saw him and didn't see him; her baby was in the back not breathing so the last thing that was on her mind was why this man was here so concerned. He watched her from across the room to the point that it made her a little bit uncomfortable. She got up out of her seat and moved to a point in the room where he could not see her and sat down again. She put her head down and again she started to pray. This time she was specific; "God I need your help, I know that you see everything and that you are in control of everything. I know too that you can make anything happen that you want to happen so Please God let my baby be O.K. Ain't that why Jesus died?" she ended her prayer with a question.

Leah dozed a little after she prayed. A few minutes later the doctor came out to tell them that Bianca was breathing on her own and he felt that everything would be O.K. Some how there had been a massive blood clot lodged in her nostril, Bianca had been crying so much that she had not been able to breathe through her mouth. The doctor said that she was a very lucky baby. He believed that all of the crying had somehow dislodged the clot causing it to start to pass. Her luck had continued when Leah noticed that she had stopped crying. The CPR that Leah had given her baby had in fact saved her life.

The doctor continued to talk but Leah didn't hear much after that. Out of the corner of her eye she could see Sgt. Windsor cup his hands to his mouth and thank God. She didn't care; she didn't even know who all was there that day. She just wanted to see her baby. The doctor was saying something about the remnants of the clot having to be removed and that the baby was resting but that she could see her. He took her by the arm and began to escort back to where Bianca was sleeping like an angel.

She just stood there and stared at her. The doctor got her attention and motioned her over to a table where he would show her the thing that had caused all of the trouble. The remnants of the clot were there in full view, "This is what we took from your baby's nose," he began to explain, "We're not sure where it came from or what caused it, but we do know that this could have turned out tragically had you not responded as quickly as you did. This thing could also have killed her in her sleep, Bianca is a very lucky baby."

Leah could not believe what she was seeing, the clot was big enough to stop her from breathing, least alone a baby and it was just what was left of it. She asked if she could pick up her baby and was granted permission. Anna and Gary came into the room just as she picked up the baby. They both hugged Leah as she held the baby, the crisis was over and Bianca would be fine. Leah just wanted to take her baby home but the doctor wanted to keep her overnight, "Just for observation" he told her, "You are allowed to stay with her in the room." He didn't even have to say that, Leah had already decided that if the baby had to stay, she was staying too.

Everyone was relieved to hear that the baby would be O.K. Leah had come out to give everybody the good news and tell them that they could go home. One by one they all gave her a hug and told her to call if she needed them. All except for Sgt. Windsor, he stayed back and talked to Gary for a few minutes and then left. Leah prepared to take the advice of the doctors and stay the night with the baby. Anna had gone home to be with Ne-Ne so Michelle came to the hospital to bring Leah what she needed and to stay with her for a while.

"Uncle Ernie said that everybody from both offices were at the hospital at some point today," she said with a smirk. "Yeah, I really appreciated everybody coming out" Leah responded unaware of the smirk on Michelle's face. "Yeah, especially that fine Cash Windsor," Michelle was mock fanning herself, "That boy is so fine it don't make no sense." "Who?" Leah asked not sure who Michelle was talking about. "Girl you know who I'm talking about, Uncle Ernie said that he couldn't keep his eyes off you today," Leah was still not sure who she was talking about. "You know, he works in the office with your brother-in-law."

"Oh yeah, that guy." Leah said showing her irritation. "What do you mean, that guy, that boy is fine" Michelle responded. "Yeah maybe, but ain't he married?" Leah asked. "Who cares, anyway I heard that him and his wife are separated, and even if they wasn't he could holla at me anytime, whooh!" Leah laughed at Michelle while she began to sachet around the room. "Girl you are so crazy," Leah told her but she didn't quite know what to do about the feelings that were rising up in her. Her mind told her that this was a married man but, everything else was feeling just like Michelle.

She couldn't help but to remember how handsome this man was, and how everyone seemed to like him. He just seemed to ooze confidence and he had the most gorgeous smile. He was the most delicious shade of brown she thought to herself, like the finest of milk chocolate, and the uniform that he was wearing complimented every feature of his athletic body. He was not a tall man but one look at him and you knew that he could get the job done, whatever "the job" was.

But he was married she reminded herself quickly shaking herself back into reality. Michelle was still going on about how fine he was and laughing about the fact that it would not matter to her a bit that he was married. Leah remembered how she had recently found out about Anna and Uncle Ernie and the devastation that information had brought to her. She had not gotten a chance to talk to Anna about what she knew and she probably wouldn't be brave enough to say anything now. Maybe it was just the way people did things, she reasoned. It didn't matter anyway because the man had not said anything to her except that he hoped Bianca would be O.K.

Leah and Michelle stayed up most of the night talking about what had happened to the baby. She couldn't stop watching her for a minute, she was afraid to fall asleep. She felt if she took her eyes off her for a minute something horrible was going to happen. Michelle had finally convinced her to go sleep by assuring her that she would stay up and watch the baby, which she did, but not for long. Bianca was her life and she knew that she would lose her mind if anything happened to her.

When she did wake up she called Fannie to tell her what had happened. She had to assure Fannie that the baby was O.K. and there was no need for her to come down to Ohio. Fannie reminded her how much she loved and missed her and the baby, and told her that she wanted to see both of them real soon. She told Leah that she would contact Jamie and tell him what had happened.

Leah found out that night that things were not going very well for Jamie and Tammy. In fact, Fannie said that Tammy was gone and that Jamie was raising the baby alone. Jamie had in fact been trying to get in contact with Leah but her Momma wouldn't give him any information as to where her and the baby were. Momma told Jamie that she would deliver a message to Leah as soon as possible but she hadn't.

Leah was surprised to hear that Jamie had been looking for her, she wasn't as happy about the situation as she might have been before. She had been forced to go on with her life without him and it wasn't as bad as she thought it would be. She knew that she still loved him but it was somehow a different kind of love. It was no longer that crazy kind of I'll do anything for you love. She told Michelle what was going on and she was angry. "Oh, now that Miss Thang done took off he gone look for you, I'd tell that negro to go fall off a cliff if I was you."

Leah understood and agreed to some extent to what Michelle was saying. Jamie had chosen Tammy over her one too many times and she was not about to go running back to him simply because she didn't want him anymore. But in the back of her mind she still missed him terribly, she still wanted them to be a family, but her life here was good. She was so mixed up. "God, what do I do now?" she heard herself ask out loud, "Please help me understand." Leah didn't get any answers that night, she fell asleep confused and woke up sure of only one thing, she loved Bianca and she would do what was best for her baby, even if it meant packing up and leaving a life she had come to love.

CHAPTER SEVENTEEN

Leah and Bianca had been home for a couple of days. Things were almost back to normal. The doctor said to keep a close watch over her and to check her every few hours to make sure that she was breathing properly. She had been doing that and all was well with her so far. Leah talked to Jamie the day after they came home from the hospital. She really felt sorry for him. He was heartbroken and devastated because of what Tammy was doing and he all but begged Leah to come home. Even though Leah wasn't feeling that same kind of love for him as before she agreed to come home for the weekend to at least discuss the possibility of them getting back together. She was washing clothes and packing for the weekend when the doorbell rang.

She looked out of the peephole and saw a man in uniform. She wasn't sure who it was so she stood there for a minute. Whoever it was looked good in the uniform. Something about the uniform made her crazy. He had his back to her so she waited for him to turn around. When she didn't open the door he did turn around to ring the bell again. It was Cash Windsor. Her heart felt as if it had fallen on the floor so she took a few deep breaths, looked in the mirror to make sure she was together and opened the door.

"Hi" was all she could manage to say looking a little confused. "Hey, I'm Cash Windsor, I hope you remember me, we met at the hospital," he was not as confident as he looked when he spoke. "Yes, I remember, from Gary's office come on in," Leah put on an award winning act of confidence knowing full well she was about to die on the inside. He walked inside the unit and took off his hat. Leah hoped that the "Oh My God" that was in her mind didn't come out verbally. "Let me take your hat" Leah said to him and he handed her his hat. Leah had to lower her gaze and look at the floor, like Michelle said this man was fiiine!

"I'm sorry to just stop by, but I have something for the baby and I wanted to make sure that she was O.K., that both of you are O.K.," he said handing a bag with a tiny stuffed animal in it. This really got to Leah, Bianca was just over a year old and this one act of kindness was more than Jamie had done since she was born. He had brought a few things to the hospital when she was born but since then, nothing. She accepted the bag and thanked him. She had to walk away because for some reason, all of a sudden she was doing everything that she could to fight back tears and she was losing. The tears started.

"I'm sorry, I didn't mean to upset you, are you alright?" he asked. "Yeah, it's O.K., I'm glad you came. This is so sweet, she is going to love this," she said as she walked toward the playpen where Bianca and Ne-Ne were sleeping, "I'll give it to her when she wakes up." Cash walked toward the playpen and watched Bianca for a few seconds, "You have a very beautiful baby girl" he said and before Leah could respond he continued, "She takes after her mother" now he was looking at Leah. She was afraid to look back at him for fear of what might happen. She was feeling pretty betrayed by her emotions and she wasn't taking any chances so she didn't look up.

"Thank you, it's very sweet of you to say that" she said finally able to glance up at him. There was a moment of terrible awkwardness, Leah didn't understand what was happening, the attraction was so thick that you could literally cut it with a knife, she could hardly breathe and she just wanted this moment to be over. "Yeah, well I can't stay," he finally said, "I have to get back to work but I just wanted to stop by and check on you guys." Leah was trapped in his eyes now, they were gorgeous and gentle and she couldn't turn away.

"Is there anything that I can get for you guys before I leave?" Now she was watching his mouth as he talked, his lips were perfect, too perfect and in that mega second she imagined him kissing her. She shook her head, not only to say no but to shake herself back to reality as well. "No thank you," she managed to say and she walked over to the couch to get his hat. He took his hat and carefully placed it on his head. Everything appeared to be happening in slow motion, the uniform was getting to her, it framed his body with excellence and the come hither cologne was not helping.

He reached for her hand, her body was definitely betraying her, God she wanted to touch him. She just wanted to run her hands over the smooth skin on his face, then his arms with all those muscles, then his chest, "Oh God please let him hurry up and leave before I die" she thought. " Thank you for coming over," she was telling him when something behind her caught his attention.

The smile had given way to a very serious look. She turned around to see what he was looking at and realized that he'd seen the suitcase that she was packing. "Are you going someplace?" he asked her glaring straight through her. "Yes, I'm going home for the weekend," she told him, she didn't know why but she was tempted to lie to him or even worse to change her plans. But she had promised Fannie that she would see the baby this weekend and promised Jamie that she would at least talk to him about coming home for good.

"For the weekend?" he asked her as if he were reading her mind. "Yes for the weekend," she repeated, "The rest of the family wants to see the baby." "The rest of the family?" he asked. Now Leah really wanted to lie. His tone made it perfectly clear that he wanted to know whom she was really going home to see. "Yes, my parents, her Dad and his parents." "Her Dad?" he asked and his gaze grew even more intense as if he were looking into her very soul to determine if she were telling the truth. The look made her uncomfortable so she looked away.

"Yes, her Dad," she finally said shaking the moment by looking back up at him defiantly. They just stood there for a minute looking at each other until Cash finally asked her, "Are you coming back?" She knew that even if she made the decision to go back to Jamie she would at least have to come back to pack her stuff so her answer was "Yes, I'll be back Sunday." "Can I call you Sunday?" he asked her. "Yes, why not?"

They both headed for the door, Cash got there first and opened it. Leah stepped off to the side expecting him to go out of the door but he didn't, he turned around putting them both in very close proximity. He was wearing Lagerfeld and standing this close to him took her breath away. She was inhaling him when he asked her, "What's up between you and Bianca's father? Are the two of you together?" he asked her. Leah did not know how to respond to that question, she knew she was on her way home to discuss the possibility of getting back together with Jamie. She knew somehow that if she said anything except the truth he would know.

She was still intoxicated by both his scent and the fact that he was standing this close to her so she still had not responded to his question. Cash reached down and grabbed her chin with his thumb and forefinger; he gently pulled her head up to meet his gaze. It was a good thing that the wall was behind her or she was sure she would have fallen. He was still waiting for an answer, this time he would not let her look away. "I'm not sure what's going to happen between us, but right now we are not together," she managed somehow to tell the truth. Cash took a deep breath and exhaled, he was no longer looking in her eyes but he hadn't moved away either. Instead he closed the door.

Leah had also lowered her gaze and was once again staring at his chest. Neither of them moved and finally Leah looked back up at his face to see what was happening. The minute that she looked back up at him he began to stroke her chin and bottom lip. His touch was very gentle so she closed her eyes. She was feeling his very breath on her face when he spoke. "When you go home this weekend," he started forcing Leah to open her eyes, "And he tries to kiss you, if it doesn't feel like this, right here, right now," he barely brushed his lips across hers, "If it doesn't feel this good, come back."

This had to stop, it was happening too fast, she was holding on with everything in her but she knew she couldn't let this go any further. She needed time to think, she needed to know who this man was and what he wanted from her. She had a million questions like where his wife was and what was going on in that situation. Reality came flooding back just as he was about to kiss her and she pushed him away. He started to laugh, "You have got to go!" she said sounding sort of desperate. "Do you really want me to leave?" he asked her. "Yes!" she said before she had time to think about how soft his lips were and how strong his arms felt. Cash smiled down at her and said "Then I'll leave, but I'm not going away forever, I'll be here when you get back," he said as he opened the door and walked out of it. He definitely had the walk of a soldier she thought to herself as she watched him walk to his car. She had a feeling that he knew she was watching but he got right into the car and drove away without even looking back.

What in God's name had just happened? She was already confused about going back to Jamie and now she felt even worse. Jamie and Cash were like night and day. Jamie was young and still struggling through a lot of emotions; Cash on the other hand was going through in his marriage but seemed to know what he was feeling and what he wanted. Jamie had changed so much and Leah wasn't sure whether or not she wanted to be a part of that change.

Leah could hardly concentrate the rest of the day. She managed to get through her packing and preparing for the weekend trip home. Suddenly, she was just not looking forward at all to the trip. Anna and Gary were taking her to the bus station and she was extremely quiet. Anna asked her if she was sure that she wanted to go at all. She let her know that she would stand behind any decision that she made.

Anna knew that Leah didn't want to go home for good. The fact that Jamie wanted her and the baby to come home was just plain bad timing. Leah was doing so well in Ohio, she had signed up for Beauty College and a management class at Wright State University. Anna wanted the best for her sister and she did not believe that included Jamie who couldn't seem to make a decision and stick to it. She and Gary argued because he wanted her to mind her own business. Anna felt that Leah and Bianca were her business and she wasn't about to let her leave without telling her again how she felt.

Anna and Leah basically agreed about the situation. Leah told her and Michelle about being confused. She was doing well, in spite of the recent drama and she knew that her life would have to change if she went back home. She would be taking care of another woman's baby. A woman that hated her guts and there was no telling how much drama that situation would bring. Jamie had to drop out of college and was barely working and she just wasn't ready for that kind of chaos. She hated the fact that she had agreed to talk to him in the first place. But so much had gone wrong in his life that she felt sorry for him. She had already made up her mind that she would go and let him see the baby, but she was coming back to Ohio.

Leah had not shared with anybody about Cash's visit earlier that day. It was just something that she wanted to keep to herself for a while. Nobody had ever made her feel the way Cash had. She just wanted to savor the moment. Who was this man? Why did he have this affect on her? She had not been able to stop thinking about him all day. She was scared to talk, afraid of what she might say. She really was confused, but one thing that she was sure of, she had to find out more about Cash Windsor.

One thing she would find out, when Cash decided that he wanted something he went after it and usually got it. He was the youngest Staff Sergeant at Wright Patterson Air Force Base and was very good at his job as assistant to one of the Colonels. He also played running back for his company's football team. He was originally from Pennsylvania, but had been in Ohio for quite some time. Cash's wife was his high school sweetheart and they had two children together. They had gotten married right out of high school and now, according to Michelle both of them wanted something else other than each other. She couldn't wait to get back and find out more.

CHAPTER EIGHTEEN

Jamie picked Leah up from the bus station with Little Jamie in tow. It was an awkward situation from the very beginning. Jamie tried to kiss her but Leah made it perfectly clear that there would be no picking up where they left off. She knew this made him feel bad, and it wasn't that she didn't care about his feelings but she had learned to care more about her own. Besides she had gone through this with him before and the end result was he always went back to Tammy.

They all went to see Fannie who was so glad to see Leah and the baby. Bianca had grown so much and she was truly a very beautiful and smart baby. Fannie adored her and throughout the night Jamie continued to look at both mother and daughter in awe. He continued to say that he wanted the four of them to go back to his house but Fannie knew Leah very well. She saw that even the mere suggestion of being alone with Jamie made her very uncomfortable. She didn't want to hurt her grandson's feelings but she loved Leah as her own and she wasn't about to let him push her into something that she did not want to happen.

In a way that only Fannie could pull off she encouraged them to stay at her place for the night. The three of them laughed and reminisced about old times. They loved and admired both of the babies. Little Jamie was also a beautiful baby, both babies looked a lot like their father and so they looked alike even though they had different mothers. For the most part the conversation was much about Leah's new life in Ohio, how well she looked, and how much she had grown up. No longer was she the lost young girl she was when she left. She had grown into a beautiful mature young woman who had dreams and goals of her own.

Jamie admired the new and improved Leah but he was expecting the Leah of old to show up. He was expecting her to run into his arms and be happy that he had decided that he wanted her back in his life. He expected that clingy young girl to step off of the bus but instead he had encountered the new and improved Leah. A beautiful young woman full of confidence and not quite as happy to see him as he expected her to be in fact, she was not what he expected at all. She was quiet and reserved and would not look him in the eye the way that she used to. Jamie convinced himself that she must be seeing someone else and he couldn't wait to get her alone so that he could ask her about it.

Leah did not want to be alone with him. Even though she knew that something was happening between her and Cash, she also knew that it had nothing to do with what she no longer felt for Jamie. He had disappointed her time after time not to mention all of the hurt that came as a result of all the disappointments. She didn't trust him with her heart anymore; she wasn't about to let him get to her again. The spark was gone out of those eyes that she used to love to gaze into so much. Life had dealt him some bitter disappointments as well and she did feel something for him; she did still love him but she realized that she was no longer in love with him the way that she once was.

They spent the night with Fannie and left early the next morning to see Momma. Momma was happy to see the baby as well and they spent a big portion of the day with Leah's family. Finally she had used up all of her excuses and she and Jamie left for his place with the kids. It was raining outside and they were happy to get inside when they got there.

There was a small bungalow that sat back off the street in between two houses. From the outside it appeared a little rundown but Jamie seemed very proud of this place. Leah stepped inside and put her bags down on the floor. The place wasn't filthy but neither was it clean. It looked like a man lived there, newspapers and clothes were littered around the place and it was very dusty. She got an uneasy feeling as soon as she looked around because there were roaches crawling around in the middle of the day. To the right was the living room but there was no furniture there, to the left was the bedroom, which had the T.V., the bed and a chair. Straight through the living room was a small kitchen with a refrigerator and stove, but no chairs.

Leah picked up her baby and stepped into the bedroom. She purposely sat on the chair and started to take off Bianca's jacket. Jamie brought their bag into the room and sat on the bed to take off Little Jamie's jacket. He moved around the room to put away the coats and the bags but he never really took his eyes off Leah. Leah on the other hand could not even bring herself to look at him. She did not want to see the hurt or the fear in his eyes. Especially since she knew that she was going to hurt him even more.

"You can't even look at me Leah, what's going on?" Jamie finally said. Leah took a deep breath and finally said, "Nothing is going on Jamie, I'm just feeling a little scared." "Of me?" he asked her. "Of this," she answered. Jamie walked over to the bed and sat directly in front of Leah, he tried to grab her hands but Leah pulled her feet up into the chair and sat back pulling her hands with her. Jamie was angry now, "All this time, this is what you said that you wanted and now all of a sudden you're scared?"

Leah looked up at him for a brief second. There it was, the tears, the hurt, and the anger, all of the things that she did not want to see. "All this time is right Jamie, it's been over a year, did you think that I was going to continue to live my life on hold waiting for you to decide if you wanted to be with us?" "You know that it wasn't like that Leah, out of all the people in my life I just knew that you would understand. You know what Tammy put me and the baby through," he was shaking his head in anger and unbelief now. He couldn't believe that things had changed so much. He was up now, pacing back and forth, going on and on about doing everything that he could to make it possible for them to be together as a family and how he could not believe that she did not want the same thing.

Leah was scared and confused; she had never seen him act this way. He was acting as if more than a year had not passed since their last serious conversation, as if he had been in contact with them on a daily basis. She wasn't sure what to say so she said nothing; she wasn't sure what to do so she did nothing. She just sat there and let him rant and rave while she held onto Bianca as tightly as she could. One thing that she did recognize and understand was the hurt that Jamie was feeling, she knew that all to well.

Jamie finally sat back down on the bed opposite Leah, "Baby, we could make this work," he told her as he took Bianca from her arms. Leah was reluctant but she let the baby go. Jamie laid her on the bed next to Little Jamie, they looked so angelic lying there, and they were so much alike that it was scary. Both Leah and Jamie were just admiring how beautiful the kids were. Once again Jamie tried to hold Leah's hands but she would not let him. The anger that she had witnessed earlier returned with a vengeance.

Jamie snatched her up by her clothes and pushed her into the wall. "What is going on with you?" he asked her through clinched teeth. "If you think for one minute that I'm going to let you just walk away with my baby you are as crazy as she is." Leah did not challenge him physically; she just stood there and began to shake her head no. When she finally was able to look up at him she was crying. "You don't want me Jamie, you want Tammy, you're not mad at me, you're mad at her. It's not me that you want to hurt it's her. I have never done anything to hurt you, I've always been on the sidelines waiting, hoping, and praying that you would recognize that I wanted us to be together more than anything. But you chose her Jamie, not just once but over and over, I had to stop hoping or lose my mind. I had to move on."

Jamie could not be believe what he was hearing, he knew that what she was saying was right and true but he just never believed that she would ever say those words to him. In his mind there could only be one explanation, "Move on?" he questioned her, "Are you saying that you are with somebody else now? Is that why we can't be together?," he was desperate for an explanation other than the fact that he had simply waited to late, put her through too much. He just did not want these to be the reasons why they couldn't be together.

Leah shook her head no once again, " I have not been with anybody else since I left Detroit," she answered him. She looked up into his eyes as she answered him. She could tell that he wasn't sure whether or not to believe her, after a few seconds he knew that she was telling the truth and he let go of her. Leah knew that at the first opportunity that she got she was going to take her baby and get out of there and never be alone with him again. But he was so angry and she had to start to figure out a way to calm him down.

She held his face with both hands and made him look at her and repeated, "I have not been with anybody else since I left, that has nothing to do with why I'm scared of us. You just have to give me a chance to believe that you want us back." Jamie took a deep breath and backed away. "So you're not saying no forever?" Leah watched as hope was literally restored to his eyes." All I'm saying is that I'm not going to run back into this before I know for sure what's going on." That seemed to be good enough for Jamie.

They had stopped on the way for food, so Jamie took the things out of the bags and they sat in the middle of the bed and ate, all except for Little Jamie who didn't eat much. When Leah got ready to go into the bathroom Jamie told her to wait a minute. He went in first Leah assumed to straighten up before she went in. She heard him make a few swats and remembered the roaches that she had seen earlier. He even made a joke about them as she went into the bathroom telling her not to stay in there to long without him to protect her. Leah never showered so quickly in her life, she then got Bianca and Little Jamie and cleaned them up as well.

Jamie was sleeping when the three of them came back into the room, Leah was glad for that. She tried to give Little Jamie some more of the food but he still didn't want it. She gathered all of the leftovers together and took them into the kitchen. It was dark and she didn't know where the light was so she just sat the food on the stove and went back into the room to make sure that the kids didn't wake up Jamie. Thank God he was still sleeping. She turned off the T.V., climbed up on the bed and pulled the babies up next to her. She didn't realize how tired she was but she must have fallen asleep right away.

From somewhere a baby's scream woke her up from her sleep. She sat straight up in the bed. There was a light coming from the living room and so she was able to look down and see that Bianca was next to her in the bed. It took only a few seconds to realize that Jamie and Little Jamie were not in bed. "So you want to play with the stove?" she heard Jamie ask Little Jamie and then another scream. Leah jumped up from the bed to see what was going on. The kitchen light was not on but Leah could see Jamie standing next to the stove with Little Jamie holding his hand near the fire. Little Jamie was screaming. As Leah ran towards them Jamie looked up at her and said, "He was in here playing with the stove so I'm going to teach him a lesson," and he started to try to put Little Jamie's hand in the fire.

Leah was petrified; she grabbed the baby from him and held him tight. Little Jamie was crying hard, Leah just stood there holding him trying to figure out why Jamie would do something like that to his own son. "No!" Leah told him, "He was just trying to get his food, he wouldn't eat it so I brought it in here and put it on the stove." Jamie seemed dazed, as he appeared to notice the food for the first time. "Oh," was all that he could manage to say.

Leah was looking at Jamie in horror, she looked down at Little Jamie's hand and saw that it was burned, no skin broken, just a little red but burned just the same. She looked back up at Jamie and caught a glimpse of the wall behind him. The wall appeared to be moving, Leah thought that it was because of the fire flickering so she spotted the light switch and reached for it. Just as Jamie said "No!" she turned on the light. Leah could not believe what she saw, a scream rose up from somewhere her voice never came from before. For a few seconds she was stuck in that spot just screaming.

Roaches began to scatter everywhere, they covered everything, literally. There was not a spot in the entire kitchen where there wasn't a roach crawling. From the biggest to the smallest they were everywhere. She had seen roaches before but never like this. She would learn later of the infestation but right now she was stuck in the spot she was in not able to run or to turn away from what was so absolutely terrifying that it would haunt her for years to come. Jamie finally touched her and snapped her out of it. She held onto Little Jamie and backed up from the doorway.

Then she remembered Bianca in the room helpless and asleep. She took Little Jamie and ran into the room. Jamie was saying something but she didn't know what and she didn't care. She didn't want to but she laid Little Jamie down on the bed. She snatched the covers off of Bianca and began to inspect the bed around her. She picked her up and began to inspect her to make sure that nothing was crawling on her. Jamie turned on the light in the bedroom. Again roaches were everywhere. Leah checked Bianca's clothes and then checked herself to make sure none of the creatures were on either of them.

Jamie had a shoe and was killing them. Leah pushed everything off of the bed so that she could see if any were there. When there wasn't, she gathered both of the babies close to her crawled into the middle of the bed and began to cry. Jamie was killing the ones that he could catch with a shoe but for the most part they were all running and hiding. When for the most part they were either dead or hiding Jamie came and sat on the bed with Leah and the babies. "I meant to tell you not to turn off the T.V. or go into the kitchen, I'm sorry this is the only place that I could find that I can afford to live."

Leah couldn't answer him. She was terrified not only because of the roaches but now she was reliving the vision of Jamie standing there holding Little Jamie's hand over the fire. She just rocked the babies and cried. Jamie tried to comfort her but she wouldn't let him touch her. "Listen, I know this is not what you expected," Jamie was saying oblivious to the fact that the roaches were no longer the primary source of her fears, "But we can find a better place if you just come home." Leah came to herself long enough to take another look at Little Jamie's hand. He squirmed when she touched it letting her know that he was in pain. She asked Jamie for a cold cloth to put on it and he got it for her.

He was trying to explain that this was not the first time that he had found Little Jamie near the stove, that he was only trying to teach him a lesson about getting to close to the stove or turning it on. None of what he was saying was registering with Leah. He was pleading with her to come home and help him with Little Jamie and to let him be a father to Bianca. The thought of him even being around Bianca when she was not there scared her, a lot, too much. She had witnessed a side of him that she had never seen before. She could only describe it as pure evil. How could he have hurt his own child? How could he put his hands on her in a violent way?

This was not the Jamie that she had fallen in love with. This was some sort of monster that had allowed his situation to turn him into the kind of man that would hurt the very people that he claimed to love. She didn't want any part of it, but she didn't want to upset him any more. She searched her heart and mind for the right words to say that would encourage him without lying to him. She had to get Bianca and herself out of this house and tell somebody what he was doing to Little Jamie. Jamie continued to tell her how things could be so different if she would just come back to him. She had heard all of this before.

"Why should I believe you this time?" she finally asked him, "What makes this time so much different from all of the other times when you swore we could be together, only to go running back to Tammy when she snapped her finger?" Jamie was desperate to convince her, "It is different this time because she is gone for good, she went to California to be with her Mom, she's not coming back." Leah's mind was racing now, if this was how he was treating her no wonder she left. Jamie wanted complete control and when he couldn't get it he got ugly. "I can't just drop everything and come back, I've registered for school Jamie, Anna needs me and I can't just walk out on her after she has been so good to me. You have to give me some time to know that this is real this time, it's only fair."

Jamie didn't want what Leah was saying to make sense but it did. He had no choice but to concede. It was daylight by the time they stopped talking. Leah got up and dressed her and the babies as quickly as possible. She convinced Jamie to leave early for the bus so they could have breakfast, but the reality was she wanted out of that house as soon as possible. They had breakfast at the bus station; Jamie was excited about making the changes he had to make in his living conditions and proving to Leah that he wanted them to be together.

Leah on the other hand could not wait to get on the bus back to Ohio. She would stop and call Fannie on the way to let her know how Jamie was treating the baby. She was afraid that after she left things would be worse for him. It was the most that she could do for him besides praying, and that she knew that she would do. She had to protect her own child, and that also she would do. No one would ever hurt her baby. She would protect her with her life if necessary.

She would never allow the things that had been done to her to be done to her baby. No one would ever abuse her. The beatings that she had taken as a child would never happen to her little girl. The sexual abuse she had suffered as a child would never happen to her little girl, she vowed to make sure of that. She had no way of knowing that she couldn't protect Bianca from everything. At this time, in her mind she would protect her baby with everything in her, in every way that she knew how. The problem she would find out would be that she didn't know how.

She got on the bus that day knowing that she was not coming back to Jamie. He was not the person that she thought he was and she knew he would never be. Leah had been reading a lot lately and she had romantic notions about how things were supposed to turn out. She didn't realize how naïve she really was but she would soon find out. Storybook endings only happened in the romance novels that she had come to enjoy so much. It would come as one of life's hard lessons but she would eventually find out. Too bad it was going to have to be the hard way. She didn't know that then. She waived bye to Jamie and Little Jamie knowing that this part of her life was over, she would go back to Dayton and begin a new life for herself and Bianca. Maybe she should have been, but she was not afraid.

CHAPTER NINETEEN

Leah tried to sleep on the bus ride back to Ohio but it was impossible. Every time she closed her eyes the pictures came flooding back. Jamie holding Little Jamie's hand over the fire, all the roaches crawling all over the house, Jamie grabbing her and yelling at her, the memories just would not stop flooding back to her. She was holding on to Bianca so tightly that she was afraid that she was going to hurt her. She decided that she would just stay awake.

She realized that she got to choose what she thought about for the most part while she was awake. Her mind moved forward back to the life she thought was waiting for her in Ohio. She had enrolled in Beauty College and was taking a business course at the local college. Not to mention whatever was brewing between her and Cash. The thought of him made her warm all over and brought a much-needed smile to her face. She had very little to smile about for the entire weekend and the thought of getting home suited her just fine.

She did not see fear and confusion when she looked at Bianca as she had seen over the weekend. She could tell that as young as Bianca was, she was happy to be away from that place and those people. She slept like an angel and that brought an even greater smile to Leah's face. The smile gave away to sadness as she thought about what Little Jamie might have to go through so she took a moment and asked God to protect him. She didn't know a lot about God at that time but Momma used to always say that "God takes care of all babies and fools" She sort of smiled when she realized that took care of both the Jaime's'.

Gary came to the bus station to pick them up, Anna was not with them. Gary told her that Anna was playing Bingo with her friends. Leah couldn't help but wonder if she was really playing Bingo or if she was really with Uncle Ernie. Gary seemed not to have a clue and she wasn't about to say anything to him about it. Gary had been around their family forever. He was really good friends with Brother and a distant cousin to Jean, another of Leah's sisters who had a different father. Leah was grateful because she always knew that she could depend on him. She had some memories of him as a little girl but she was so messed up back then that it was hard for her to recall most of what was going on back then. She just remembered Gary always being there for Anna even when she had other friends. He was good to her and Leah appreciated him.

She didn't share everything with him but she did tell him about the roaches. Gary laughed, as he was the one to tell her that the house must have been literally infested and probably needed to be bombed, Leah laughed and told Gary, "Yeah, with him in it." Gary suggested that she leave her bags in the garage to air out in case there were any of the critters still lurking in the corners of the suitcase somewhere and she did just that. She was happy to be home to her own bed. Her nieces and nephew were happy to see her and she was happy to see them. All in all it was a good homecoming.

Leah took a shower and bathed Bianca. Then she went about her regular Sunday routine of getting her and the kids ready for the week. Anna had come home and wanted details about Detroit and Leah gave her the skinny on everybody that she had gotten a chance to see. They laughed for hours about her ordeal but even though Leah was laughing, part of her was very sad about the way things had turned out between she and Jamie. She was very happy and lucky to have a caring home to come back to and she knew it. She appreciated Gary and Anna more than ever before.

She was pretty tired so she took Bianca up to their room to lie down for a while. She was lying there waiting for Cash to call her but somehow fell asleep. She had the phone extension right beside her but still somehow she did not hear it when it rang. Gary had answered the phone when Cash called and told him that she was sleeping. Cash told him that Leah was expecting his call but Gary refused to wake her up. In fact Gary let Cash know that night that even though he could do nothing if Leah decided to pursue a relationship with him, he was not convinced that it would be in her best interest to do so. He didn't want her hurt and he made that very clear.

Cash and Gary were good friends and Cash felt that he could speak honestly with him. He let Gary know that although they were friends and he respected him as such, he was right, there was nothing that he could do if the two of them decided to pursue what they were feeling and he had every intention of doing just that. He asked Gary to let Leah know that he had called and said goodnight. Gary was not angry but he was concerned.

Although Cash and Leah both knew that something was happening between them it would be weeks before they would actually act on how they felt about each other. They would talk on the phone a few times, see each other at a party or a game, but Leah was careful not to fall in as she had done with Jamie. She watched him from a distance. Uncle Ernie played on the same football team and she would go with Michelle under the guise of supporting him.

But the reality of the situation was that she loved watching Cash and somehow she thought he knew it. The games were not supposed to be full contact, in fact it was a flag league but these guys were serious about their football. He had a reputation for breaking through lines, going around guys, under them, over them, whatever he had to do to get the ball across the goal line and the other teams defense looked forward to messing him up.

They had not really had a chance to talk so Leah still did not know what was going on between him and his wife. She and Michelle came to one of the play-off games to watch them play. Leah was feeling good that after this game they would finally get a chance to talk. Win or lose he had told her they were going out afterwards for a drink. It was a great game very close and very intense. Their team had been unbeatable during the regular season and was the odds on favorites to win the championship. Leah and Michelle were having a lot of fun watching the game and the guys, all of them.

The flirting was something that she was beginning to enjoy. Cash didn't like it at all and he shot her a few looks into the small crowd to let her know that he didn't approve. This game was different from the others. It was just electric, their team was winning but by a very small margin. Michelle was doing most of the yelling and flirting with the other guys, but Leah was enjoying herself as well. Michelle knew that Cash didn't approve of the flirting that they were doing but Uncle Ernie and Gary thought it was funny.

Cash seemed to focus more on the game now and pretend that he didn't really care. It had been very hard the last few times he had gotten the ball. The other team anticipated every move that he attempted and stopped him dead in his tracks each time. Leah was concerned now because she saw that he was getting frustrated. He really ignored her now and Leah began to wonder if she had gone too far with the flirting. Finally, he got the ball, found a small opening, got a great block and was off to the races. Everybody stood on their feet and cheered as he put the game a little further out of the reach of their opponents.

"Uh Oh," she heard Michelle say as Cash made his way back to the sideline. "What?" Leah asked her. She followed Michelle's gaze and saw a young woman and two young children making their way to the sidelines. She had seen this woman before, she didn't know who she was then but the woman seemed to know who she was. They were at the local gas station and Leah had spoken to the woman at the time and put her out of her mind.

It didn't take a rocket scientist to figure out who she was at this point. "That's his wife," she heard Michelle say, but she had already put two and two together. She was not unattractive and appeared quite intelligent and her children were beautiful. The young boy was a smaller version of his Dad and the little girl looked just like her Mom. Leah couldn't take her eyes off of what was taking place, the young man ran over to Cash on the sideline and Cash picked him up and hugged him. Then the little girl ran over and hugged him. The exchange between husband and wife was no more than a nod but Leah could tell that there was a lot behind that nod.

Cash shot Leah a different kind of look this time. She wasn't really sure what it meant but it felt sort of like the satisfaction of seeing her confused. Leah didn't like the look one bit so she made it her business to continue to flirt with the other players. She knew somehow that this was getting to him but she also knew that he either couldn't or wouldn't say anything to her about it in front of everybody. She wished that he would, but she understood and respected why he didn't.

When the game was over his kids ran over to congratulate him. So did a lot of other people but Leah stayed back. She didn't know what to expect and she didn't want a scene so she watched from across the field while she pretended to be interested in what one of the guys from the other team was saying. She caught a glimpse of Gary watching her but gave him a look that told him she was O.K. Eventually Cash headed for the parking lot without even looking her way. She was crushed down on the inside but she wouldn't show it. Michelle came over to console her, "I don't know what's on his mind but it's his loss'" she said to her, "Let's go over to the club and have a drink."

Leah was still watching him, she believed that he knew it but he wouldn't even turn around to acknowledge her. He motioned for Ernie to come over to him and whispered something in his ear. Ernie smiled and said something back to him. Leah could see his arrogance even from where she was across the field as he made a final remark to Ernie before walking toward the parking lot holding his daughter's hand. She didn't need to see anymore, this made her uncomfortable. She turned to Michelle and said "Let's go."

The game had been at a small community field that was walking distance to both of the local clubs. Both of the clubs were civilian run, one was a local bar called "The Joint," and the other was a VFW club affectionately called "The V" by the locals. They were deciding which one to go to when Ernie approached them. They both shot him a look that said he was the enemy. He laughed and told them, "Don't kill the messenger." His laugh gave way to a very serious look and he said "Seriously, he wants you to go home, he says he'll call for you in a while." "Bull#@&*!," Michelle said, "That Neggah can't have his cake and eat it too, let's go Leah."

Ernie gave Michelle a concerned look, "Stay out of this," he warned her. Leah looked across the way at her brother-in-law. She could tell that he was concerned but he didn't say anything. He just shook his head and looked away. Leah knew that he didn't like the idea of her getting involved with his friend, but he had never said anything negative about Cash. She wanted him to say something but what he said only confused her more. "I'll see you back at the house," saying without saying that she should do what he said. As Gary was walking away she looked back at Ernie, he looked her in the eye and said, "I've known him for a long time baby, don't cross him."

The words, both spoken and unspoken cut like a knife. Michelle spoke up and said, "Cross him my foot, what about him crossing her?" It was a valid question but Ernie just shook his head and reminded Michelle to stay out of it. Leah and Michelle began walking; Michelle was going off on all three of them, Gary, Ernie and Cash. Three peas in a pod she called them. Leah decided that she would walk to "The Joint" with Michelle. Not in defiance of Cash, though he would take it that way, but just to have a drink and clear her head.

When they got there the club was busy as usual with both military and civilians, including a young man who was staying in the housing area with his brother and sister-in-law. Leah had seen him around and he had even introduced himself to her as Leon one day at the park but she wasn't interested. Now here he was offering to buy her a drink and without thinking about the implications she accepted. Michelle was in rare form, she and her boyfriend were not speaking and she was playing the field like a natural born fiddler. The young man came back with the drink and proceeded to talk to Leah, she didn't want to be rude but she couldn't stop thinking about Cash, and she really just wasn't interested in anything he had to say.

She reasoned that she didn't want Cash to be mad at her for nothing, and since there was no one at the club she was interested in she excused herself from the young man and went to say bye to Michelle. Michelle called her a woos and promised to call her later. When she got to the door the young man offered her a ride home, she declined telling him that she needed to walk and started home. As she was walking she noticed the young man drive by and assumed that he just wanted to make sure that she got home alright. About half way home she saw a car slow down out of the corner of her eye. She assumed it was the young man again so she didn't even look up.

She heard the electric window come down and Cash say "Well, if isn't the life of the party. Cash's car was very distinctive, in fact there was only one other one like it in the area. It was a two toned Buick Electra and he looked very distinguished driving it. Leah looked up at him but didn't say anything. "Where are you going?" he asked her. "Home," was all that she could make herself say. Just then the young man pulled up next to Cash, he looked past him and asked Leah if everything was all right. She told him that it was and he sped off.

"Who is that?" Cash asked her. She had started walking again and he was riding along side her. She told him that it was some guy from the club. "I thought you were supposed to be waiting for me at home?" Leah kept walking without responding. She wasn't sure what was going on but she didn't like the way that he had treated her at the game. If in fact he and his wife were not together then why did he ignore her that way? She kept walking. "We need to talk," Cash said still riding beside her, "Get in," he commanded.

Leah didn't like his tone, "Go home and talk to your wife." "Look, don't go there, just get in the car." Cash responded. "Leave me alone" she told him. Cash stopped the car, put it in park and stepped out. Leah turned around to face him. "Get in the car so we can talk, please." Even the please sounded like a command but Leah knew she had to face this thing sooner or later so she decided to get into the car. Cash pulled off and had not gotten a half block when the traffic light stopped him. He looked over and much to his surprise there was the young man next to him at the light. He glared at Cash so he let down the window, "You got a problem?" he asked the young man. He didn't respond he just looked straight ahead and pulled off quickly when the light changed.

Cash turned his attention back to Leah, "Don't be out here walking by yourself," he commanded. "You sure are used to barking out orders, I'm not one of your soldiers and I'm not your wife," was Leah's response. Her comments cut but Cash knew that she was angry and perhaps even hurt. He recognized that she was trying to piss him off so he took a deep breath, smiled and kept driving. He drove her down into the heart of the city, into a real neighborhood something Leah had not seen since she moved to the military base.

He pulled up into the driveway of a house Leah would find out belonged to yet another friend of his. This was an older guy who had retired from the military and decided to buy a home in the city. He was married and had been for a very long time. "I don't want to visit anybody," she told him. "We can talk here," was his response. He got out of the car and walked around to Leah's side to open the door. He reached for her hand, she just sat there, "Please" he said and she took his hand and got out of the car. Lilly, the woman of the house met them at the door, "You must be Leah," she said with a big smile.

"James is in his room watching T.V., I'll get him" Lily told them. Leah looked around to see an immaculate home with pictures of family members young and old. There were pictures of Cash and his family, and lots of other relatives and friends. Cash was about to say something to her when James walked into the room, "Well, look—a—here, who we got here?" James asked already knowing who she was. He seemed genuinely happy to meet her. Cash did the formal introduction and told James that they were just going to hang out for a while. James and Lilly opened their home up to them, which seemed very strange to Leah since they obviously knew that he was married. Who were these people and why was everybody so loyal to him? James and Lily excused themselves leaving Cash and Leah alone to talk. Leah couldn't stand the pictures so they went into the den to talk.

"Sit down," Cash told her. She didn't want to but his voice did this thing to her that just caused her to give in. She sat down and so did he. He sat back against the couch and put his arm behind her. She sat up immediately, "What do you want Cash?" He held her arm so that she couldn't get up, even though she didn't really want to, "I want you, I want us." "You are a married man," she was getting anxious. "Listen to me, I'm not going to lie to you about anything that's going on with me, I love my family," Leah tried again to get up but he wouldn't let her.

"I love my kids, but Carla and me been over for a long time," Leah didn't want to hear anymore, she tried to get up but he wasn't about to let her go, this was the talk they had avoided for a few of weeks now. He knew that if he didn't say everything that he needed to say tonight he would never get another chance. "Please, please listen to me." Leah sat back. "Yes, I'm still married, you need to hear this from me, I even still live there for the most part, as far as the Air Force is concerned but I spend most of my time here. I've been trying to do something for the past year that my heart is not in, I've tried to keep my family together, and even before we met it was hard. Now it feels like it's impossible, I can't think, I can't sleep, all I can do is think about you."

"Leah, I can't make you any promises, but we need to find out what this thing is between us. Baby I'm no angel, I've been with other women, but nothing like this, you make me crazy. Every body is saying that I should leave you alone, and maybe they're right but I don't want to, I'm not sure I could even if I did want to." Leah was putty in his hands. He was being completely honest with her, something Jamie had never done. It felt good to hear him say that he wanted her. It wasn't about him being good looking; he was mature and respected and oh my God, why was she doing this again?

She found the strength to get up and walk to the other side of the room. He didn't try to stop her this time. "I know too that you are still dealing with what happened with Bianca's father. I don't know what he did to you and right now I don't even care," he stood up, walked across the room to where she was, and put his arms around her. "Let me tell you what I do care about," he touched her face and tried to make her look at him but she wouldn't so he snuggled her neck with his nose, "I care about taking care of my kids and I care about finding out what this thing is between us, period."

Leah couldn't fight him anymore; she laid her head on his chest and gave in. Cash took a deep breath and held onto her tight. He kissed the top of her head, then her forehead; he took another breath and kissed her eyelid then her nose, Leah realized that she was not breathing, she couldn't. Cash held her face in his hands, forcing her to look at him, they just looked at each other and at that very second, she knew that nothing else would matter. There was still a very small voice somewhere warning her but she didn't listen. She shook her head to try and gain some perspective on what was happening but it was too late, "Cash?," she didn't even know what she wanted to ask him. "What" he answered her just about the time that his lips touched hers.

His kiss was both deep and gentle at the same time. "What?," this time his response was a challenge. He kissed her again, this time neither of them held back anything. Leah had waited a long time to be kissed this way. She and Jamie had done the whole deed and it didn't feel half as good as this kiss. He could have stopped right there and her body would have been more satisfied than it had ever been with Jamie. But he didn't stop; he touched her in places that she didn't know would make her respond. The small nibble on the back of her neck, and on her ear lobe, while all the time caressing her back. She was this close to losing her mind, now he was kissing and biting the front of her neck, and finally back to her lips.

Her body exploded, "Oh my God!" she moaned. Cash stepped away from her; he held onto her hand and walked her down a short hallway into his room. It was true; all of his things were there, his uniforms, his shoes, and the MVP trophy that he had won at the banquet last week, all neat and immaculate a far cry from Jamie's place. She had just stepped into another world and she was sure that she loved it. Cash had his back to her as he pulled his shirt over is head. The sight of him without a shirt made her crazy. His neck, back and arms were extremely muscular, and this time she was not going to stop herself from touching him.

Something arose in her that she did not recognize. She didn't wait for him to turn around, she walked over and put her arms around him, he was a little stunned but didn't stop removing his clothes. Something had taken over her and at the same time there was something missing. The thing that was missing seemed to increase the passion in her. He took off her clothes and she let herself go, no guilt, no inhibitions; that's what was missing. Every time a man had ever touched her in her life there had always been something to feel guilty or tense about. With Brother and Pa-Pa and even with Jamie she had always kept herself from enjoying it because it was always something wrong attached to it.

But this was different; it couldn't be wrong, it felt too good. She had never felt this free, out of control, and in control all at the same time. Cash was passionate, intense, thorough, and articulate. After tonight she would forever know the difference between having sex and making love. Cash was a master at the latter, she gave herself to him completely, she had no way of knowing how this man's intensity would come back to haunt her in other areas of her life. Why didn't somebody tell her that she would live to regret this night? She probably wouldn't have listened anyway. Why didn't somebody warn her that the things that he would teach her would forever affect the way that she dealt with men? In essence; the prey would soon become the predator.

CHAPTER TWENTY

For the next few months, Leah's life would be fun and exciting. She was enrolled in school and doing very well. Everything in her life seemed to be going really well. Cash was very attentive; Bianca's health was great, and she was on her way to as normal of life as she had ever known. Or so she thought. She had met new friends at school, which was good for two reasons, Michelle could not stand the hold that Cash had over her friend and she and her boyfriend had gotten really close so she and Leah didn't hang out much anymore. Leah was grateful to Michelle though because she stepped in to watch the girls while she went to school.

Michelle had always been a good friend to her though; she said what was on her mind freely. Leah had learned to ignore the things that she said about Cash for the most part, but she was glad to know that she had a friend that would tell her the truth no matter what. Michelle wasn't the only one that didn't like what was going on between Cash and Leah, Anna had done everything including threatening him to get Cash to leave her sister alone but nothing had worked. She had even set her up with Will from her office who was handsome and single but that didn't work either. Leah thought that she was in love. She also loved the part where she for the most part got to do whatever she wanted, go wherever she wanted, whenever she wanted. For the most part Cash could not say anything to her publicly because he was still married.

She had learned to use that against him and it drove him crazy. Cash had taken a part time job at the "V," mostly for the money but he was a party guy. He liked being where the action was. Leah was pretty, sexy, and popular by now but no one at the "V" would come anywhere near her because they knew she "belonged" to him. For the most part if she came into the club it would be to piss him off by flirting with a non-regular. She did that often because he couldn't do anything about it, or so she thought.

This particular night Leah came to the "V" with her new friend Sarah. She was in a show off mood and wanted Sarah to see first hand how Cash reacted when she flirted with other guys. They had already been to the clubs down in West Dayton before they got there so they were well on their way to more than a little tipsy. The second that Cash looked at her he wanted her to leave. He made his way over to their table to take their orders for drinks, "What are you ladies having?" he asked staring directly into Leah's eyes as if to send her some subliminal message that he was not in the mood for her foolishness tonight.

It was the very look that she was looking for. She had come to get some sort of sick pleasure out of seeing him squirm in public. They gave him their order while Leah made it her business not to look him in the eye for long. She knew that she was going to ignore his subliminal orders and have some fun flirting tonight. Cash went back to the bar to fill their orders. His friend and Sgt-at-arms of the club, Nelson, walked over to him as he was pouring their drinks. The two of them exchanged knowing looks and began to laugh. "Man" was all that Cash could say through the laughter. He actually paused for a minute and enjoyed a moment of laughter using it to get himself focused on what he knew was about to happen. "Man!" was all that he could manage to say.

Nelson put his hand on Cash's shoulder and asked if he was going to be O.K. "I guess we will soon find out" was Cash's respond as he finished pouring the drinks. "Let me take the ladies their drinks" Nelson volunteered. "Yeah why don't you do that" Cash responded. To the surprise of both men when Nelson turned around to take the drinks over to the ladies they were already being joined by two Staff Sergeants who were there for training from Washington. They both began to laugh as Nelson headed over to the table.

"Hey Nelson" Leah acknowledged him as he sat down the drinks. "Ladies" Nelson responded as he put down the drinks, "Are we behaving ourselves tonight?" "You wouldn't have it any other way now would you?" Leah said as Sarah flirted with Nelson. The two guys sat back appearing to know that there was something going on but unsure of what it was. "How much do we owe you?" Sarah asked not knowing that Leah never paid for drinks at the "V." "This one is on the house" Nelson told her, "What can I get for you gentlemen?" he asked the guys.

As Nelson took the drink orders from the guys Leah picked up her drink and feigned a toast toward Cash who lifted his glass toward her from across the room. He had the same threatening look in his eye, the one that told her she should behave. She had been trying him a lot lately, making him jealous every opportunity that she got. He had been allowing her to get away with it so far but he was quickly growing tired of her childish games. They continued to look at each other from across the room; there was so much passion between the two of them that the guys could not help but notice. They ordered drinks for the ladies and excused themselves from the table.

When Cash saw the men leave the table he felt a sense of victory. He reasoned that Leah knew that he was not in the mood for her usual behavior and had taken heed to his non-verbal warning. Leah in fact had decided by the way that he was looking at her that maybe she should not push him tonight. They were still looking at each other when somebody said "Hey Carla" which brought them both out of their trance. They both looked at Carla and back to each other before Cash made himself look away and at his wife.

Something Leah would later recognize as reality clicked in her spirit. It was as if someone had stabbed her through the heart. She sat there as stoic as she possibly could afraid to move or say anything for fear of what she might do or say. Cash was afraid as well; he glanced at her every opportunity he got to make sure that she wouldn't do or say anything crazy. Sarah didn't have a clue.

All kinds of things went through Leah's mind and she at least considered them all. She thought that she might say something to him, or perhaps her. Or even to ignore them both and seek out the one of the soldiers that was in the house from Washington but decided against all of the ideas that were flooding her mind. What she really wanted to do was to find someplace to run and hide but her pride would not let her resort to what she deemed cowardice. One thing was for sure was that for this moment in time she was definitely in the wrong place. The guys were going out of their way to be respectful to Carla, that's how they operated. She became invisible to all of Cash's friends except for Nelson, who was yet worried about what her reaction would be.

Nelson made his way over to the table where Leah sat alone for the moment. Sarah was on the dance floor really enjoying herself with no idea what was going on. Nelson sat down at the table with her and for a brief moment did not say anything. He and Leah exchanged looks and at that moment she was very grateful to find out that he was not only Cash's friend but hers as well. He reached across the table and grabbed her hand. No other friend of Cash's, not even Ernie would have had the nerve to touch her not even in this situation, but at 6 ft 8 in tall and 310lbs there wasn't much that he was afraid to do, especially for a friend.

"Are you O.K.?" he asked her. "I'm good" Leah lied, "I'm not going to do anything stupid if that is what you mean, I do think that it is time for me to leave though." "How about one for the road?" he asked her. "That would be good" she told him as he got up from the table to go to the bar. Leah looked out on the dance floor at Sarah, she was having a ball. Leah didn't want to spoil her friend's fun but she knew that she had to get out of there.

As she stood to go to the phone she felt many eyes on her. They expected her to clown but she had decided she wasn't going to give them the satisfaction. Even Carla watched her as she crossed the room. Carla was far from stupid, she knew exactly who Leah was and that she and Cash were seeing each other. Leah knew that she was watching and she moved across the floor with the greatest confidence. As she passed by Carla she couldn't stop herself from meeting Carla's gaze as she continued on to the pay phone. Woman to woman the look told Carla that she was not intimidated by her presence but that was far from the truth.

She finally made it to the phone but when she dialed her sister's number she got no answer. Now she would have to figure out another way to leave gracefully. It would have been so good for her to go back to her seat, gather her things and head for the door knowing that her sister only lived minutes away. Now she would have to come up with another plan. She stood there at the phone for a minute contemplating what her next move would be. She sensed someone walking toward her and turned around to see Carla headed her way.

She took a deep breath and braced herself for the possibilities. Over Carla's shoulder she saw Cash stop Nelson from approaching the two ladies. "Hello" Carla feigned politeness. Leah greeted her with that same fake hello. "You are Anna and Gary's little sister aren't you?" Carla asked already knowing the answer. "I sure am" Leah answered her with her offenses up. "Tell them that Carla, Cash's wife said hello" Carla said sarcastically. "If I see them before you do I'll be sure to do that" Leah replied with the exact same sarcasm. Not knowing what to do or say Carla continued walking toward the ladies room. Leah stood at the phone smoldering, she looked up and directly into Cash's eyes, his look defied her to do anything crazy.

She decided against acting out not because of the way that he looked at her but because she wasn't going to give him the satisfaction of seeing her clown. She also loved Anna and Gary and didn't want to do anything else to embarrass them. It was bad enough that she was involved with a married man she didn't want it to get back to them that she had actually ended up in a fight because of him, especially not with his wife. She took a deep breath and headed back to the table where she was sitting. Sarah was back at the table and Leah took the opportunity to bring her up to speed on what was happening.

"What do you want to do?" Sarah asked. "I don't want to spoil your fun, I'll be O.K." Leah told her. "Are you sure?" Sarah was drunk and having fun and had heard just what she wanted to hear before some guy drug her back onto the dance floor. Leah sat there nursing her almost empty drink. The urge to run had morphed into something else, a calm cool reserve. She sat back and took in the scene. She watched as Carla came out of the ladies room, went to the bar and asked her husband to dance. He tried to discourage her but she wouldn't take no for an answer. Leah smiled to herself as she realized that Carla was doing everything that she could to get a rise out of her.

Leah was smiling, looking down into her drink for a brief moment. She heard someone say "Hey Will" and that made her look up. She was pleasantly surprised to see Tech Sgt. William Peterson standing not far from the entrance to the club. It was Will from Anna's office whom Anna had tried to fix her up with. They had spent a weekend together in Cincinnati for the Riverfront Jazz Festival. They had ended up leaving early for two reasons, number one; she just wasn't feeling him because she was so caught up in Cash. Secondly, when he tried to have sex with her she had discovered that he was an abnormally large man, which had scared her tremendously. Remembering the incident had made her smile and look away.

About the time that she looked back up, he spotted her and started to walk toward her, straight to the table. "Hey beautiful, I know that you are not here alone" he said to her. "No, I'm with a friend" she told him. Will worked closely with Anna, he knew about Cash and Leah, he had heard all of the talk and it didn't take him long to access the situation and realize that Leah was in a bad space. He knew that he couldn't be her man but he had told in times past that they could always be friends. He understood and respected the fact that she could not simply turn off her feelings for this man but it did not stop him from wanting her to see the situation for what it was and be with him.

"Give me a hug girl" he said and Leah stood up and hugged him. Cash and Carla were on the dance floor and she really couldn't tell which of them was more interested in the sudden appearance of this gorgeous man that had joined her. They both knew him, everybody did. Most thought that he was weird, he was into Karate and self-discipline, and was very quiet and reserved. He was not a womanizer and did not do the club scene too often. Most could not understand why he did not have women hanging off him, but Leah did.

They spent a lot of time talking the weekend of the festival, Leah had been honest with him, not only about how she felt about Cash but also about the fact that he was more than she could physically stand. He shared with her his gratitude for her honesty and also the fact that most of the women he had attempted to get physical with usually got scared. The difference was that they would never talk to him about it; they would just stop accepting his calls. He always knew that this was the reason and had grown to view himself at first as somewhat of a freak. Eventually he had gotten into Karate and self-discipline so that he could learn to control not only his emotions, but also his sexual urges as well. What everyone else thought was weird Leah knew was the way that he protected his feelings.

In any case she was glad for his sudden appearance and the company. "I see that you're still hanging in there with the madness," he said as he took in the scenario. "Yeah" was all that Leah could muster up to say back. Will watched the people on the dance floor, which included Cash and Carla; he nodded to hello to Cash. "Girl, what are you doing?" This ain't cool, why do you insist on…" he stopped what he was about to say when he looked at Leah. "What do you want to do?" he asked her.

"I wanted to leave but my friend is having so much fun, I didn't want her to have to leave to take me home." "Down the street?" he asked her, "She could have come right back if she wanted to keep partying, I'm scared of some of the people that you call your friends. You mean she knows the deal and she didn't pull you up out of here?" "She don't know how bad it really is" Leah defended Sarah. Will was looking at her like he wanted to choke some sense into her. "Do you still want to leave?" he asked her. "Yes, I think that I do."

"Listen, personally I don't care what he thinks about you leaving with me, I can handle him even on your behalf if you want me to. But what is he going to say or do to you if you do leave with me, can you handle that?" Will was genuinely concerned. "I'm not talking about leaving with you and going someplace to be with you Will; I'm just asking if you would take me home" Leah responded. "That wouldn't make a bit of difference to me if I was him, all I would see is you leaving with another man because you don't like the situation that you agreed to be in from the beginning"

"Well he's just going to have to deal with it because if you will take me I'm going home" Leah was angry. "Because you want to tick him off or because you want to go home" Will demanded to know. "Like you said, what difference does it make, he's going to believe what he wants anyway." "It makes a difference only because if you are just using me to make him mad at least be honest enough to tell me" Will told her. "That's not what I'm doing; I was trying to leave even before you got here, honest." Will just looked at her for a minute. The music had changed and Cash and Carla were leaving the dance floor. Will did not like the look that Cash shot his way so that helped to settle the matter, "Let's go" he finally told Leah.

"Just let me tell Sarah that I'm leaving" Leah said as she made her way to where Sarah and Nelson were flirting heavily with each other. As she approached them Nelson gave her a concerned look. "Are you sure you are O.K.?" he asked her. "Yeah, but I'm going to get ready to leave" she told him. "With Peterson?" he questioned. "Yeah, I'm just going to let him take me home" she explained. "You know that you gone have to deal with him about this one?" he asked her knowing that she had weighed the situation. "Yeah, and I will. I'll see you guys later."

Leah turned around into one of the most intense looks that she had ever gotten from Cash. He looked as if he literally wanted to kill her, she would not return his gaze. She didn't want him to think that she was blatantly trying to defy him but she had to go. She walked back over to the table and picked up her purse. Will sat there for an extra second and having witnessed the look Cash had given her asked her again if she was sure she wanted to leave with him. Leah was tired of the games; this had been the ultimate slap in the face for her.

Cash had actually expected her to sit quietly in a corner somewhere until he could get back to her. She had felt the sting before of not being able to publicly show their affection but it was never this bad. All of a sudden she wasn't sure she could handle the relationship as it was. Cash watched every move that she made. She was more than aware of his gaze but she had made up her mind. There was no turning back she knew they would fight. In some ways she knew this was the beginning of the end but she didn't care. She felt she had to draw her line in the sand.

She felt his stare burning a hole through her but she kept walking out of the club. Just as she walked by him she did look over to say goodnight to everyone in his direction. He was angry and she knew it but she kept right on walking. There was such a relief for her when they finally went through the door. She took a deep breath and walked with Will to his car in silence. She was more upset than even she realized, she wanted to cry but she fought back the tears. Will opened the door and let her into the car. By the time that they had driven the few blocks to Anna's house Leah realized that she was not ready to go in. When she hesitated to get out of the car Will noticed and so he pulled off again.

He drove them to the NCO club on base. It was a smaller crowd there so they got a booth and ordered drinks. Will did not want to drill her about what she was feeling, he pretty much knew. He kept quiet until Leah started to talk. She felt so stupid; she should have listened to her sister. She never should have gotten involved with him but it was too late. Now what was she going to do. She kept talking until the tears came. Will didn't say anything he just let her talk. He just sat there and watched her fall apart; when his heart couldn't take anymore he scooted around and held her while she cried. As a friend, he knew at this point there was no chance for the two of them but he wasn't going to abandon her. She needed a friend and he would settle for being that friend tonight.

Leah finally was able to stop crying. They finished their drinks and left the club but not before some of Cash's so-called friends had seen them together. Friends who couldn't wait to tell him what they had witnessed at the club. Leah didn't notice them and she probably wouldn't have cared if she had. By morning Cash would know that she had been to the club with Will and that he had saw fit to comfort her in front of everybody. On top of everything else, he would not be happy about this. Even though nothing had happened between them there would be hell for her to pay in the very near future. She was ready.

CHAPTER TWENTY-ONE

Cash was livid. He had called several times since she had left ending up waking both Gary and Anna. Needless to say they were not too happy when Leah finally made it home. They told her that he had been calling and was very mad. Anna was really mad when she found out what had happened. She was angry at Cash, she felt like he was taking advantage of her sister. She was even angrier with Leah for being so stupid. She had talked to her until she didn't have anything left to say but nothing she said mattered. She knew that this thing had to end and she didn't see it ending peacefully.

Gary and Anna had gone back to bed when the phone rang again. Leah answered on the first ring. Cash was angrier than he had ever been with her before. The thought of another man touching her made him crazy. It was evident, it was 3:00 a.m. and he was calling from the phone booth on the corner. "Where have you been?" he asked so angry that it seeped through the phone. "I wasn't ready to come home so we went to the NCO club for drinks" Leah was being honest but it wasn't helping. "Right, open the door," he demanded. But Leah was not about to open the door for him, nor was she going anywhere with him which was his next suggestion. She knew that he was angry enough to hurt her and she wasn't about to take the chance that she would not be able to reason with him that night.

She told him to go home and that they would talk about it tomorrow. Cash did not want to agree but he had no choice. Leah had finally stood up to him and it felt wonderful. For months she had wanted to loose the hold that he had on her. She had been walking around blindly agreeing to everything that he said. She would not even consider anything anyone else was saying. Anna and Michelle had been telling her for months that she was a fool, but she really believed that Cash loved her.

He had to didn't he? I mean he made her feel things that she had never felt before. He wanted to be with her, she didn't have to chase him around town like she had done with Jamie. He came looking for her. What about the things that he told her? He didn't care about his wife, did he? He had to be telling the truth. Why else would he be running around the streets at 3:00 in the morning trying to find out where she was? If he wanted his wife he would be at home with her right now.

Above everything else that caused her to believe that Cash loved her was the intimacy that they shared. They could make love for hours fall asleep and wake up and do it all over again. It wasn't just the sex or was it? For the first time Leah allowed that thought to creep into her head. Cash had taught her so much about how to please him. It was second nature now. Sometimes they didn't even talk, she knew those days when the office or his family situation had gotten to him and she just wanted to make him forget about everything and everybody except her, and she did.

She remembered something that he had said to her once, "The thought of you being with another man makes me crazy," now she wanted to know if it was just that he didn't want her to be intimate with another man. Not because he was willing to go through whatever he had to go through to be with her to make her his wife but because he wanted that "chick on the side." That "other woman" that he could just go crawl into bed with and make the rest of the world disappear. "No!" she heard herself say out loud just before the tears returned. This could not be true, she couldn't be that stupid.

Cash had made two mistakes that night. He had shown Leah that once again she was not a part of his real world, only a hidden one that included the two of them. She was right back where she started, Cash may have been a little more sophisticated at playing the game than Jamie was, but it was the same game. Leah cried silent tears that night. She was hurt and humiliated. She could have gone upstairs and told her sister that she made a mistake and asked for her help or better still called Michelle. She knew that either of them would have been willing to comfort her and help her get through this revelation but she was too embarrassed to ask for help. The second mistake that he had made was to show her that it really did make him crazy to think that she was with another man.

The pain was so bad that she thought she would die. She refused to feel it so she did what she knew would numb the pain; she went to her sister's liquor cabinet, took a big drink and laid back down. She pulled Bianca close to her and began to drift off. The last thought she had that night was that if she found out that Cash was lying to her he would have to pay. She was going to make sure he felt the same pain that she was feeling if he wasn't telling the truth. She had to find out and she would. She finally drifted off to sleep.

CHAPTER TWENTY-TWO

The next morning Leah had a terrible hangover. She went into automatic pilot mode, helping the kids get ready for school. She bathed and fed Bianca and Na-Na and put them down to play. She went about her morning chores as usual. As soon as she sat down to have a cup of coffee the phone rang. She knew that it would be Cash; she was surprised that he waited this late to call. The first thing that he said to her when she answered the phone was, "Why did you let him touch you?"

"Good morning to you too," Leah said to him. "Man, forget that, why were you letting him touch you?" It wasn't so much anger that she heard in his voice now. He had definitely calmed down and now Leah was sure that she heard hurt and confusion. She recognized it because it was the same things that she had felt last night. "Cash you know that I would not let him or any other man touch me, not the way you're saying," Leah told him. "You shouldn't have been with him in the first place, I should have been holding you last night Leah," Cash sounded desperate.

"I won't even ask how you know he was holding me," It was Leah's turn to be angry now, memories of the waves of anger and humiliation came flooding back to her. Her head was already about to explode from the hangover so the memories made it even worse. She wanted him to feel what she had felt and she knew how to make that happen. "No," she finally said, "You were exactly where you should have been, with your wife." "Baby please I'm sorry about what happened last night," Leah cut him off before he could go any further, "Me too" and she hung up the phone.

Cash called right back, "Please tell me that you did not just hang up on me on purpose." "I don't have anything to say to you Cash," she told him. "Well I got a lot to say to you, I'll meet you for lunch." Leah had already decided that she wasn't going anywhere that day but she did not tell him. Between the hangover and the embarrassment she just could not face the people of Page

Manor. Not long after she hung up from Cash Michelle showed up to get the girls so that Leah could go to school. She took one look at Leah and knew that something was wrong.

Michelle knew that Cash had done something, she loved her friend but she had no sympathy for her where Cash was concerned. She made up her mind in that instant that she wasn't even going to ask her what was wrong; she made a conscious decision to talk about something else. "Me and the girls are going to the park today for a while, then to the zoo," she finally said. "You don't have to take the girls today Michelle, I'm not going to school" she said almost at the point of tears. Michelle had never seen her friend this sad before, she had to know what Cash had done. Leah had made coffee so Michelle poured a cup and sat down. She continued to watch her friend go through the motions of the morning looking as if she wanted to die.

"It's O.K. if you're not going to school, I'll take the girls anyway you look like you could use a break" Michelle said still not wanting to talk to her about Cash. Leah knew that Michelle was going out of her way not to ask her what was wrong and that made her feel even worse. This was her best friend, the one she could talk to about anything but she felt that she couldn't talk to her about this. Michelle had teased and encouraged her in the beginning but when she found out what was really going on in this man's life she warned Leah to leave him alone. "Yeah he is fine, and if the sex is that good go ahead and get you some, but don't fall in love with him" she had advised her friend. But it had been too late.

Leah felt like dying, she didn't respond. Michelle finally couldn't take seeing her friend in pain anymore. "What is he doing to you?" she finally asked. Leah could not hold back the tears anymore; she let go and told Michelle what was going on. "I am so stupid, why didn't I listen to you and Anna?" Leah went on to tell her what happened the night before, even as she repeated the story she knew that it wasn't over between her and Cash, she knew they would fight but she also knew that somehow they would be together again and so did Michelle. Michelle just shook her head, "Girl, you need to..." she stopped herself from saying I told you so, it wouldn't do any good anyway. Her friend was hopelessly in love with this man and she was going to have to find her own way out of this. "I'm gone go ahead and take the girls" Michelle told her, and she did just that.

Michelle gave Leah a big hug before she left. She told her that she loved her and would support her in whatever she decided to do. She reminded her that she didn't think that being with Cash was the right thing for her but she stopped dead short of saying that I told you so. Leah appreciated Michelle's honesty and loyalty and told her that she would call her later when she decided what she was going to do. They both knew what she was going to do, at least today. Michelle said good-bye and left with the girls.

Leah went back to trying to cure her hang over. Then the thought came to her. She used to hear her mother say it all the time. "A little hair of the dog that bit you," so she went to the liquor cabinet and took a drink. She knew that she was going to see Cash so she made an extra effort to make sure that he didn't smell the liquor on her breath. She took a long hot bath, prepared her skin with Cash's favorite perfume and lotion, put her hair just the way he liked it and waited for his call. It did not take long. Cash had gone up to the school looking for her, someone had told him that she didn't come to school today and he had gotten angry all over again.

The call that Leah had been waiting for came, "You couldn't pick up the phone and tell me that you weren't going to school today?" That twisted pleasure that Leah got out of making him crazy was back. "I knew that you'd find out soon enough," she responded. "Girl, I swear to God you...where are the girls?" he asked her. "They're with Michelle, your number one fan," she told him. "I can only imagine what she said to you about me" he shot back. Leah was annoyed, "Contrary to what you believe every conversation that I have is not about you." That comment cut as deep if not deeper than Leah intended, "Whatever, I'm at the "Joint," I'll be there in a few minutes to pick you up."

Leah got a little scared, he didn't sound like he was mad enough to hit her but he was definitely still irritated. He was only down the street so to calm herself Leah had another drink. He got there quickly; too quickly Leah was not done brushing her teeth for the third time that day. He tapped on the horn once but she kept doing what she was doing. By the time she rinsed her mouth and came out of the bathroom he was at the door. The screen was locked so she unlocked it and stepped toward the couch to get her purse and jacket.

Cash thought that she was still playing games with him so he stepped inside the unit and grabbed her arm. He pulled her back toward him until he could reach her neck. Cash grabbed her neck with the other hand and pushed her against the wall. He looked her square in the eye and said, "You really need to stop playing with me." Leah had a look of total defiance in her eyes that made him even angrier. "I was in the bathroom," she finally said to him, "But by all means go ahead squeeze, you can't hurt me anymore than you already have." Her words felt like a punch in the face. Cash softened the grip he had on her neck; the grip was immediately replaced with stroking. He tried to kiss her but she moved. She knew they would end up making love this afternoon but it would not be easy for him and it would be on her terms.

She got her purse and jacket from the couch. When she turned around again Cash was still leaning against the wall. He knew that he should leave but he couldn't. "I'm ready," Leah told him, and they both walked to his car. Cash's focus was off; instead of him taking her to his room in the city he drove right back to the Joint. He took her to a booth in the back of the bar and they sat down. Leah swung around sideways and put her feet on the seat with her back against the wall. She was so damn sexy all that Cash could do was to sit there and look at her, but she would not look at him. When she finally did look up she looked right into the eyes of Leon who motioned her a toast from across the room.

He was so weird she just looked at him. Cash looked across the room to see who she was looking at. "Who is that fool?" he asked her. "Nobody" she answered, still not returning his gaze. She knew the effect that her not looking at him was having and she was enjoying every minute of it. Cash looked at his watch, he had spent most of his lunch tracking her down. He didn't have much lunchtime left but he wasn't about to leave now. "I have to call the office and let them know that I'm not coming back today; do you want a drink while I'm up?" Now she looked at him, she didn't answer him she just looked at him. "I'll take that as a yes" he said as he walked away.

Leah watched him as he walk away; he was so handsome. God, she had to be with him today. She watched him walk over to the phone and make his call. He was so intense; she figured that he was lying about where he was to his secretary. She watched as he went over to the bar to get their drinks. She loved watching him and he knew it. While his back was to her Leon walked over to the table, "He leaves you alone a lot" he said immediately making her skin crawl. "What do you want Leon?" she asked him irritated that he had stepped into her view of Cash. "I just wanted to tell you that if you were with me I would never leave you alone"

"That's nice to know Leon; but I am with him and you should probably leave us alone," she told him wanting him to leave before Cash turned around. "I'll do whatever you want" he said, "Whatever you want," he repeated. She was so creeped out that she just watched him as he walked away. Cash was coming back to the table with their drinks, when she saw him moving toward her gaze shifted to him. He had seen the way that she was looking at Leon so she shot a look his way as well. He looked back at Leah, she didn't want to look at him but she could not take her eyes off him.

Cash and Leah were so into each other that neither of them paid attention to Leon arguing with the bartender. Cash sat down in the booth and told Leah that he had the rest of the day off. "Drink up" he told her, "We're going to the city." Leah was just looking at him now; she was more in love with him than she had ever been. Cash was just as into her as she was into him at that moment; he just wanted to be alone with her, to make the rest of the world go away. He reached across the table, took her hand and kissed it. Every ounce of anger in both of them disappeared. Cash took a deep breath and closed his eyes. "I feel like I'm losing you." He seemed so desperate at that moment, "I'm right here Cash, and I'm not going anywhere," she told him.

But before he could respond to what she said Leon walked up to the table. They both looked up at him. "Leah this is a peace offering, I wanted to say that I'm sorry for making you mad." Cash and Leah looked at each other. Neither of them could believe that this guy would have the nerve to come to their table while they were talking, especially not bearing gifts. Cash responded with controlled anger, "Man, take your drink and go while you still can." "You should not keep leaving her alone" Leon said taking his eye off Leah for the first time since he had approached the table and staring defiantly at Cash.

"What the fuck is your problem?" Cash asked him standing up now. Leah grabbed his arm to pull him back down, "Cash just let him go." "He'd better do just that, get this shit and get away from us," Cash told him knocking the drink onto the floor. The bartender came over yelling at Leon to leave. Between the angry bartender and the look on Cash's face Leon decided that it was time for him to make his exit and he did Cash snatched his arm away from Leah and glared at her, "What's going on Leah?" he asked standing over her as if he wanted to hit her. She just looked up at him, she couldn't believe that he was accusing her of him, "With him?" she questioned, "Cash give me a break."

"Come on man, the guy is just weird," the bartender said snapping him back into reality. Cash calmed down, he was angry with himself for losing it the way that he had. He apologized to Leah and to the bartender. He sat back down in his seat; he couldn't believe the emotions that were going on in him today. He took a couple of deep breaths to try to calm himself down. He had always been able to master his emotions; no woman had ever gotten to him this way. His fists were in balls and Leah reached out to try to hold his hand but he wouldn't open it. For the first time in his life he felt conflicted.

In his mind he didn't want her to touch him, to have this kind of control over him. In his heart he didn't know what he would do if he couldn't feel her touch. His body craved her he couldn't let her go. He opened his eyes and looked at her; she mistook the look and let go of his hand. He grabbed her hand and again started to kiss it. That quickly his mind was made up, he was not about to let her go. "Let's go," he finally said. He seemed to have calmed down again so Leah grabbed her purse and jacket and walked toward the door with him.

Once outside they immediately spotted Leon sitting in his car. Leah held onto Cash's hand tighter. He walked her to the passenger side of the car and opened the door. Leah didn't trust that he was not going to start a fight with Leon so she looked him in the eye. "I'm not going to do anything to him" Cash responded to the look. He helped Leah into the car and closed the door. He walked around the back of the car and opened the trunk. Leah got back out of the car to see what he was doing. "Get back in the car," he told her calmly but she didn't she watched him.

Cash took a small box out of his trunk, opened it, looked inside, closed it and walked around to the driver's side door. "Get back in the car," he said to her again as he got into the car. Leah took one last look at Leon who was still sitting there eerily watching them, then got back into the car. Cash opened the small box and took out an automatic weapon, he removed a clip from the box, held it up so that Leon could see and put the clip into the weapon. When he was certain that Leon saw what he had done he lowered the weapon and removed the clip. He then pulled out of the parking space and directly in front of Leon's car, he paused there and looked Leon in the eye. When Leon finally looked away Cash pulled out of the parking lot and headed for the city. Leah turned around and watched as Leon got out of his car and headed back toward the bar.

Cash told Leah to put the box under the back seat and she did. Once the box was put away Leah moved closer to Cash. They both seemed to take a deep breath grateful that their angry ordeal was over. Cash glanced over at Leah and she kissed him then laid her head on his chest. Just as they both seemed to settle down they heard the sound of the police siren. Cash looked in his rearview mirror and saw the police car coming up behind him. He assumed that they just wanted to get by so he pulled over. They were not that lucky, the crazy ordeals of the day continued. The police car pulled up behind them and the two officers jumped out of their police car.

"Driver, step out of the vehicle hands first!" one of the officers said guns drawn while the other officer pointed his gun at Leah. Leah and Cash looked at each other both knowing what this was about. Cash complied immediately and was made to lie on the ground. Then Leah was asked to exit the vehicle and she also complied. The officers handcuffed them both and stood Cash up. When they asked if he was carrying a weapon he said yes and told them where it was. He also informed them that he had a permit for the gun and told them of he situation, which caused him to remove the gun from the trunk in the first place. The officer informed him that there was a complaint against him for garnishing a weapon at a citizen. Both Leah and Cash began to laugh.

Right about then another squad car pulled up, he called the officers over and they consulted with each other. The officers walked back over to Cash smiling. "You're in luck," he told him handing back his driver's license and gun permit, "The bartender at the Joint just confirmed your story, we're going to have to ask you to return the gun to the trunk." The officers began to remove the cuffs from them both. Cash looked over and asked Leah if she were all right and she told him that she was. "We do apologize to you and your...is this your wife?" the officer asked him. "No, she is a friend," Cash responded. "We apologize to you and your friend" the officer was being sarcastic now.

Cash and Leah got into the car and headed for the city once again. This time Cash didn't waste time; he started the car and pulled Leah close to him. He apologized to her for all that had gone on and promised to make it up to her. Once at the house they both took a deep breath. They didn't fall into each other's arms as they thought they were going to, instead once alone the atmosphere became very awkward. Cash still had something to say about her leaving the club with Will last night. He needed her to understand that she couldn't just take off like that with other men.

"The smartest thing that you did last night was not to let me see you," he told her holding her face close to his. " I don't ever remember being so mad in my life, I really wanted to hurt you." "What about how hurt I was last night Cash," Leah interrupted, "How do you think it makes me feel when you and all of your friends ignore me when she comes around?" "Listen, I've never lied to you about my situation, she is still my wife and I have to respect that baby, I don't want her to have to go back to Pittsburgh with the kids. This way she can continue to stay in base housing and you and I can be together. If I make waves she's going to take my kids and go back to Pittsburgh and I can't deal with that."

"This is not right," Leah told him, "It's not fair that when she's around I have to watch the two of you act like a normal married couple, but the minute that I even look at somebody else you want to fight, I just don't know if I can keep doing this Cash." "Don't talk like that Leah, don't say that, when you say stuff like that it makes me crazy. I'm not with her like that Leah; I don't look to her for anything except to be the mother of my kids. Everything else I share with you," Cash was pleading his case now, "I know that it has to be hard to watch but know this; at the end of the day you're the one that I want to be with, you're the one that I'm going to be with if it's possible. Don't do that, don't run off with somebody else baby and look to them to comfort you. I could have made you understand if you had just…"

"Just what Cash, sat around and waited until you got done playing husband?" Leah asked. "No," Cash told her, "waited for me to make the situation right so that we could have been together instead of you being someplace else with somebody else letting them comfort you. I can't no I won't deal with that ever again. If you ever feel the need to do that again just know that I'm done, because I can't be responsible for the way that I react to that situation."

Leah looked him in the eye, "There you go threatening me again." "I'm not threatening you, I just need you to understand how it made me feel for you to leave with him last night, and then for my friends to tell me that you were hugged up with him in a public place. What would you have done if the shoe were on the other foot? When everything was over I walked her to her car and sent her home, I just knew that you were at home waiting for me.

How would you have felt if I had left with her last night, if I had comforted her in public?"

Leah walked away from him, "I'm tired of her reminding me that she is still your wife." "When did she say that?" Cash asked her. "Last night." Leah answered. Cash walked over to hold Leah again, "Stop letting her get to you like that, you know who it is that I want to and am going to be with if you give me the chance." He was tired of talking; he snuggled closer to her and began to kiss her neck. All of the fight was gone out of Leah, she couldn't have resisted him even if she had wanted to and she didn't want to. The kisses were as deep and as passionate as they had ever been allowing them once again to shut out the entire world and spend the evening comforting each other as if they were the only people in the universe.

CHAPTER TWENTY-THREE

The next few months was one fight after another between Leah and Cash. It became more and more difficult to shut out the world when they got together. Everywhere that Leah went she was viewed as the home wrecker. Women hated her because she was involved with a married man and men wouldn't touch her because they didn't want a problem with Cash.

But Leah had learned that just the thought of her being with someone else really upset him. Now in areas where she used to feel so powerless she had now become empowered. She'd learned to use her sexuality to get him to do whatever she wanted. If he didn't respond soon enough or the way that she wanted him to Leah would either withhold sex from him or, go out and blatantly flirt with other men in front of him. She knew that no one that he knew would get involved with her, or so she thought, so she would flirt with the new soldiers, which there were always plenty of.

But that kind of empowerment did not last long. Once Cash figured out what she was doing he began to call her bluff. He believed that she loved him and would never do anything to hurt him. He told her that she was a spoiled brat and that he would not continue to give in to her the way that he had been. Leah was starting to feel desperate. She wanted Cash to divorce his wife and marry her but he made it very clear that the separation was as far as he was willing to go at that point.

The worse part was that they all traveled in the same circle, they all knew and socialized with the same people. This was the part that was starting to get to Leah and the reason that she felt she had to try to force his hand. She had to either make him decide to divorce her or find out for sure that it wasn't going to happen so that she could move on. She was so naive, not only had Cash told her that it wasn't going to happen in every instance that the three of them had encountered, Cash had respected his wife enough not to flaunt their relationship in front of her. Leah should have felt the same way but she did not and Cash was growing tired of her always making a scene.

He really did love Leah, but it was becoming clear to him that she was not mature enough to handle the situation and he was going to have to take some drastic measures. He had tried to break up with her on several occasions but it had not worked. The minute that he would see her, hear her voice or even her name he would start to miss her. He kept trying to stay away but found that it was impossible for him to do. The last time that he had gone back t o her he told her, "I have tried, but I just cannot stay away from you."

Armed with that confession Leah was determined that she was going to make him really choose whom he wanted. She'd picked the occasion where they would all have to see each other. Uncle Ernie was having a birthday party for his wife and they would all be there. Of course Carla would be there, she and Sheila were friends. In Leah's mind this would be the night that changed things for them. She had no idea how right and at the same time how wrong she was. Uncle Ernie and Sheila had made her promise to behave and she did promise. She wasn't planning any trouble or anything like confronting him in front of everyone. No, she wouldn't confront Carla or anything stupid like that, she had only planned to do what she did best and that was to make him jealous.

Cash knew that Leah would not be able to get through this night without some kind of drama. He also knew that by the time that this night was over he would either be through with Leah or she would have to grow up and accept things the way they were for now. He knew that she would do something stupid but he was not sure what it would be. He took his time dressing that night. He not only wanted to look good but he wanted to appear to be in charge of the situation. Carla had stopped seeing whomever it was that she was seeing and was now hoping to have her husband back, and he knew that she was also capable of bringing drama.

He shook his head as the possibilities of what might happen tonight crossed his mind. He didn't believe that Carla would act out without provocation. She had told him as much when he warned her not to act out. She was more mature and had the leverage of still being his wife, for now. It was Leah that he was worried about; there had been something about her demeanor even as she looked him square in the eye and promised that she would behave. Cash took in a deep breath, released an even deeper sigh, checked himself in the mirror one last time, and left for the party.

Carla was on a mission of her own. She wanted her husband back and was ready to fight for him. She wouldn't dare challenge Leah physically; the girl was young, fit and desperately in love. She would not hesitate to rise to the physical challenge so even though she was sure that she could take her if she had to, she would not be the one to initiate physical contact. But Carla was refined, in some ways elegant with the distinct advantage of still being Cash's wife.

She pulled out a few pieces that she knew used to get Cash's attention, but they were what she called wife clothes. This was another area that she could not compete with Leah in. Even she had to admit that this girl just oozed sexuality even if she was wearing a potato sack. She chose a dress that Cash had never seen her wear, the dress was black with a neckline that suggested that here was something worth seeing underneath, and a split that hit just above the knee showing her still beautiful legs. She decided against stockings, put on some strappy sandals, and touched up her hair and makeup. She was very pleased with what she saw in the mirror and she left for the party.

Leah had been preparing for this party for days. She had dieted and exercised over the past few weeks in an effort to look exquisite when she walked into the party. Now today was the day, she had decided on the perfect dress. Cash had paid for the dress site unseen, "You want me to pay for something that you are going to use to torture me with," he had commented. Leah knew that everybody expected her to wear something risqué, something that would show off all of her new curves but she had decided against it, at least in the way they were expecting.

The sales lady had brought her the dress to try on; when she put it on in the dressing room it felt different. She pulled the dress on over her head and breast and it literally fell the rest of the way down hitting every curve just right. The dress had a high neck, which closed with three snap hooks in the back, no sleeves, and an oblong opening in the front that exposed a glimpse of her cleavage. It was made of a slinky black material, gathered slightly at the waist and flowed downward across her stomach, hips, and bottom into an airy a-line hem that stopped just below the calf. It was simply elegant, a word that would become a part of Leah's ever growing vocabulary.

She stepped out of the dressing room to take a better look, the sales woman and the other women standing around encouraged her that the dress was perfect, and it was. It was definitely different than anything that she had ever worn, it was grown-up. Now here it was the day of the party and the thought of putting on the dress made her feel just that, grown-up. She had spent the day at the salon getting her hair, hands, feet and eyebrows done, a short sassy haircut, perfect eyebrows and bright red polish on her hands and feet. Outwardly she was ready but inwardly everything was shaking.

So many thoughts were going through her mind; Cash recently told her that he was tired of her being so immature. She was still planning to harass him tonight if he ignored her even though she'd promised that she wouldn't. Now something was telling her that if she did that tonight she would lose him. She wasn't sure what to do at this point. She'd been extremely quiet all day; you'd have thought that her very life depended on what happened at this party. She'd already taken a long hot bath and had a couple of drinks in an effort to calm her insides but it wasn't working. She didn't want to already be drunk when she got to the party so she decided against another drink, but she did go to her stash, grab a joint and take a couple of puffs which seemed to do the trick.

Leah combed her jet-black hair, which was a rendition of how the white soldiers wore military cuts, cut close around the sides and long on top. The hair cut itself was enough to cause a major controversy, she applied her Fashion Fair make-up that included the vixen red lipstick to match her polish. Leah started to laugh when she looked at herself in the mirror. This was certainly going to get everyone's attention. They all hated her anyway; this would really give them something to talk about. The minute that the thought came to her mind she got a little sad. The truth was that lately instead of the sick sense of empowerment she used to feel when she knew that someone was judging her there was a feeling of sadness.

Maybe she was growing up, maybe she was tired of her own childish behavior, maybe it was the fact that every time she and Cash fought lately he reminded her of how immature she was. "Grow the f#@* up!" had become as a catch phrase for him when they argued. Maybe it was a combination of all of these factors she didn't know but something was definitely changing. Leah walked over to the closet to get her shoes and dress. Even the shoes were different than anything she had ever bought, one band across the top of the shoe and a strap around the ankle, definitely grown-up. "Is it the weed?" she asked herself laughing and talking out loud to herself.

Anna stepped into the room; she too looked perfect for the party.

Tonight she could not lecture Leah about acting out, as she was herself going to her wife-in-law's party. They had joked about it earlier. Anna swore that the affair was over between she and Ernie but Leah still saw the way that they looked at each other when they were in the same room. "Are you in here talking to yourself?" Anna asked her. "Yeah, but I'm not answering myself," Leah responded and they both laughed. Anna almost cried when she saw how beautiful and grown-up Leah appeared, "You look absolutely beautiful," Anna told her. "So do you Anna," Leah told her. "No really, I don't think that I have ever seen you this kind of beautiful, Cash is going to drop dead on the spot when he sees you," Anna told her thinking that it was what she wanted to hear.

"Well I hope not," they both laughed Anna had come into the room to warn Leah about acting out tonight. She expected to find her same old rebellious little sister but instead she had found a grown up more mature version of her little sister. "What, you don't want him to fall dead on the spot?" she asked. "No, maybe just take his breath away for a few minutes," Leah joked, "No really I am tired of fighting with him all the time, I won't give him any reason to get mad at me tonight. Anyway he said that if I start anything tonight it's over." "Oh no not again!" Anna joked. "No I think that he was serious this time Anna, he really is tired of all the drama," Leah told her.

"Both of you should be tired, but I'm not going to fuss at you tonight. I want us both to have some fun tonight. Remember, there will be lots of single men at the party tonight, just keep an open mind," Anna told her. "I will," Leah lied; she had no intentions of paying any attention to any other man tonight. She'd promised herself that she would not make Cash angry tonight and she would do her best to keep that promise. She was going to act like an adult tonight if it killed her. "Do you want to walk around to Ernie's with us?" Anna asked her. "No you guys go ahead, I'll be around in a few minutes," Leah told her.

Anna left and gave Leah a few more minutes to finish dressing. Leah took a deep breath and put the dress on. The minute that she looked at herself in the mirror she knew that things would be different tonight. She looked and felt different, her thought process was different; for the first time she wasn't feeling insecure. For the first time she allowed herself to think of the possibility that maybe things were not meant to be between her and Cash.

She didn't feel as if she couldn't breathe because of the thought as she usually did. She knew she would be O.K. She took one last look in the mirror and left for the party.

Anna and Gary had stopped along the way to talk to the neighbors and so Leah was able to catch up to them. Anna took one look at her sister and almost cried, "Wow, look how beautiful you are!" Gary agreed, "I think I'd better go back home and get my gun," he joked. "Oh be quiet," Leah told them. Gary pulled the ladies to each side of him, put his arms through theirs and continued walking the rest of the way to the party. He was very proud to have the two most beautiful women in Page Manor on his arms. Leah was grateful that she had caught up to them; all of a sudden she did not want to make a grand entrance into the party as she had originally planned.

Gary felt her nervousness and assured her that everything was going to be fine. They all went into the party together; Anna was the first one to go in. Everyone was genuinely happy to see her. As soon as Leah walked through the door she spotted Michelle and made a beeline for the kitchen where her friend was standing. "Ohhhhh, look at you, girl he's going to kill you before the night is over," Michelle told her. "Don't say that, is he even here?" Leah asked. "Yeah Uncle Ernie got him working the bar, and Carla is here too. She's all dressed up like I have never seen her before, she's trying to pretend like she's not paying him any attention but she can't keep her eyes off him. You know what, I hate that you got so caught up in him but tonight, I see what you see, that boy is fine," it took Michelle all of fifteen seconds to give her the low down on what was going on at the party. "Don't look now but here he comes," she said motioning over Leah's shoulder.

Before Leah could even respond Cash was grabbing a hold of her hand. "Hey," he said finding himself lost in her eyes. "Hey to you," Leah said. "Michelle your Uncle is looking for you," he told her still looking at Leah. "Yeah right, I know when I'm not wanted, you all play nice O.K.," Michelle said as she walked away. Cash took a deep breath, "Let's go outside for a minute," Cash told her as he led her out of the back door. Once outside he turned toward her and grabbed her other hand, "Look at you, I almost didn't know who you were, damn," he said leaning his forehead on hers, " I just want us to leave."

"You know that we can't do that," Leah said wanting to leave as much as he did. "No we can't," he said, "But are you going to be O.K. tonight? You know that Carla is here?" Cash asked her. "Yes and yes," Leah said. Cash was nuzzling her face with his nose now, "We are going to be together tonight after the party, know that, no matter what, O.K.?" "Yes," Leah told him as he kissed her face. Cash kissed her lips and told her that they should get back inside and they did. That was the first time that she saw Carla. "Oh, that's where you went," she said to Cash. "Yeah what's up?" he asked her. "I was just wondering, but I should have known," she said giving Leah a dirty look over Cash's shoulder.

"We're not going to do this tonight Carla," Cash told her. "I guess we aren't going to do anything anymore," Carla said with an obvious slur in her voice. She'd obviously had too much to drink. Just as Cash was about to say something else to her Leah stepped in front of him. "I'm going to go in and say hello to Ernie and Sheila and let you guys talk, I'll talk to you later," she told Cash. Leah turned around to face Carla, "Carla," she said with a confidence that Carla wasn't going to be able to shake tonight, then she walked past her. "Leah," Carla said as she looked in her husband's eyes knowing that she no longer had the upper hand.

Leah walked into the other room with a smile on her face, for the first time she knew that Cash meant it when he said that he wanted to be with her. No matter what Carla said or did tonight she knew where Cash's heart was. She realized that he had an obligation to respect his wife and that was O.K. She also realized that Carla was probably hurting tonight, especially since she had broken up with the guy she'd left Cash for and she sympathized with her. She knew that Cash could handle the situation and she would let him do just that.

Leah went to say hello to Ernie and Sheila as she told Cash she would. Sheila was impressed with how mature Leah was acting. Her friend Carla on the other hand was getting drunk and making a fool of herself. She was all over Cash reminding everybody that would listen that he was still her husband. Sheila felt sorry for her friend; there were two things against her that she knew of. One was obvious to everybody and that was that Cash was in love with Leah.

The worst thing that was against her was that she had been with another man. Even Sheila knew how proud Cash was when it came to his women. He had to totally possess them. No other man could be able to say that he had her. Even Leah didn't know the significance of that or she wouldn't keep trying to make him jealous. Sheila shook her head as she watched her friend fall completely apart. She was pretending to be the life of the party but it was plain to everyone that she was miserable. Sheila kept expecting Leah to say or do something but at last glance she could tell that Leah felt sorry for Carla.

Carla was doing everything that she possibly could to make sure that Leah and Cash did not get to spend a minute alone. It wasn't until she had to use the restroom that they were able to steal a moment together. Once again they went out back to talk, they held each other for a moment without saying anything. Finally Cash told her, "I'm not sure what I'm going to do with her tonight, I've never seen her act like this before." Leah could tell that Cash was confused; her heart ached for the predicament that he was in. Everything in her wanted to act a fool and force him to make a choice but more than that she did not want to add to the pressure he was already feeling.

She hugged him close and took a deep breath. She didn't believe what she was about to say herself, she looked up at Cash and told him, "Do whatever you have to do for her tonight, she's hurting and feeling desperate and I can't blame her. She's been your wife and the mother of your children and now that is being threatened. I haven't loved you nearly as long as she has and I know how the thought of you being with someone else makes me crazy, I can only imagine what she must be feeling tonight. I'm going home," Cash was shaking his head no, "I'm going home, alone. That is where I will be when you're done with whatever it is that you have to do tonight. Just call me and tell me what you decide to do."

Leah was not going to let him see her cry. She was fighting back the tears with everything in her. "My decision is already made Leah, you know that I will see you tonight when this is all over," Cash was saying when Ernie came to the door and told them that Carla was making a scene asking for them. "Go on in," Leah told him, "I'll talk to you later." Cash went into the house. Leah could hear Carla talking loud and asking where she was. She decided not to go back in, not that she was afraid of Carla but because she did not want to cause a scene. She peeked back into the door to try and get someone's attention to let them know that she was leaving but everyone was watching the situation with Cash and Carla.

Leah wanted to come in and at least go out the front door but she knew that would only add fuel to the flames. She wanted to get her bag but decided to call back when she made it home to tell Anna to bring it home. Leah decided to go ahead and walk home. She didn't want to walk through the back way even though it was a short cut to Anna's house. It was either grass and hills or walking behind the garages. She wasn't afraid; Page Manor was a very safe place to live, but it was kind of humiliating to have to walk home alone in the dark shadows. But she had vowed to herself that she would not make a scene tonight and she was going to do whatever it took to keep that promise so she started walking.

CHAPTER TWENTY-FOUR

Back at the party all hell had broken loose. Carla was really clowning. She'd started crying and begging Cash for another chance. She told him that the other guy didn't mean anything to her and that she was sorry for ever letting it happen. This only reinforced in Cash's mind that he wanted nothing more to do with her. She had betrayed him and had sex with another man. He didn't think that he would ever be able to forgive her for that. But he would not abandon her in front of all of these people. "Let me take you home Carla," was all that he could manage to say to her. This was enough to calm her down. She went around the party and apologizing to everyone. In reality she was really looking for Leah so that she could rub in her face that once again Cash was going to come to the aid of his wife and there was nothing that she could do about it.

But Leah was on her way home, after attempting to walk on the grass and getting her heels stuck a few times she had decided to walk on the sidewalk which led behind the garages. She was pretty pleased with herself. To her surprise she was not feeling anxious about what was going on at the party with Cash and Carla, she knew that Cash would take care of it and come to see her later on that night. She was looking forward to it. She was planning to make it a night that he would never forget. She was deep in thought about the things they would do to each other later. That's probably why she never heard Leon step out of the shadows behind her.

"So here you are alone again. I keep telling him not to leave you alone like this." Leon said jarring her out of her thoughts. She turned around to face him. The minute that she saw him she was immediately afraid. He had a demonic grin on his face and his eyes were like something out of a bad horror movie. "Hey Leon," she tried speaking to him politely but she could see that small talk was not what he had in mind. "Hey yourself," he said walking toward her, now she could see that he was cupping something in his hand.

"You shouldn't be out here alone," he said as his hand moved slightly and she heard a clicking sound. Her eyes immediately moved to the source of the sound just in time to see the blade.

Back at the party Carla was taking her time making her rounds to say good night to everybody. She'd spotted Leah's bag and was convinced that she was around someplace. She wasn't about to leave until she could confront her with the fact that she'd won again. She had stopped acting out by now. Cash had told her he was taking her home and he was a man of his word. She knew that once he got there he would want to make sure that the kids were O.K. and her plan was to do whatever she had to do to keep him there. Whatever happened, Miss Leah was not going to see him tonight she would make sure of it. She finally got up the nerve to ask Michelle, "Where is your girl?" Michelle was not a fan of Cash's but she liked Carla even less. She could see straight through what she was trying to do. "She's not in my pocket," Michelle told her, "But as soon as I see her I'll be sure to tell her that you're looking for her."

From across the room Cash heard the exchange between Michelle and Carla. He realized that Leah had not come back into the house. He didn't know what to make out of it. He looked around the party but there was no sign of her. She must have left but it didn't matter, he would see her very shortly. As he walked across the room to tell Carla the he was ready to go he spotted Leah's bag on the sofa. For some reason this bothered him more than it should have. He made it across the room and told Carla that he was ready to go. When she walked away to get her things Cash asked Michelle, "Have you seen Leah?"

Michelle ignored him. "Please Michelle, you see what's happening I just need to know if she's O.K." For the first time Michelle became worried as well. She hadn't seen Leah for about thirty minutes and she told Cash so. Michelle went to the front door to see if maybe Leah was standing out front but she wasn't. Michelle found Anna and Gary inside the party and asked them if they had seen her and they had not. Michelle was angry now; she assumed that wherever Leah was she was upset. She spotted Cash talking to Uncle Ernie and went over. Their conversation was about where Leah could be as well.

"When did you see her last?" Michelle asked him. "We were out back talking," he answered, " I came back inside because Carla was looking for me, she told me to come in and see about Carla. She was fine she said she was going home to wait for me. I at least thought that she would come back in and say goodnight." "Well she didn't," Michelle was mad, "How could you let her just leave like that by herself Cash, Man you ain't right and I hope she see that after tonight." Ernie wanted to say something to his niece but he realized that what she was saying had some truth to it, so did Cash. Ernie went over to the phone and called Anna's house but there was no answer.

Ernie's first thought was that Leah had gotten upset with the situation and left with someone else. Knowing Leah though if she had done that she would have made sure that everyone at the party saw it just to start a fight with Cash. Something wasn't right. Just then Anna came over to Ernie, she had purposely avoided him all night but now she wanted to know what was going on with her sister. Ernie didn't know, nobody did and everybody was worried. Cash came over to them, "I'm going to drop Carla at home and stop by your house," He told Anna, "She should be there by now, I'll have her to call around here." Anna agreed to wait for the call; it would only take a few minutes she reasoned. Cash and Carla's unit was just a few minutes away. Everything was going to be fine.

Leah backed up but Leon lunged forward grabbing her by the neck, pushing her into what turned out to be his brother's garage. In the same instant he put his hand over her mouth and told her not to scream. With the other hand he showed her the knife. Leah was petrified, tears began to stream down her face as she looked in his eyes and realized that he very much intended to hurt her. "Don't cry," he told her, "This is going to feel sooo good," his voice was thick with lust, and he was touching her with his tongue all over her neck and face. "I'm going to take my hand away from your mouth," he told her, "If you scream I will cut out your tongue." She knew that he meant it so she stood still. At that point she started to think about how she could get out of this alive. She couldn't let him do what she knew that he was planning, but she had no idea how to stop him.

She tried her best to block him out as his hand started to move over her body. He reached down and pulled up her dress. Leah started to cry out loud, "Please Leon don't do this," she begged him. "Please Leon, Please Leon," he mocked her, "That sounds so good to me, just to hear you say my name, ooh this is going to be so good." He moved her away from the wall to try and force her to lie down. Leah was moving too fast trying to find an opportunity to get away so he stepped behind her and grabbed her around the neck.

"If you try…," was all that he got out before Leah stomped on his foot, grabbed his testicles and snatched away from him. He let out a loud scream as he let go of her. She maybe got two steps away from him when he grabbed her again. She tried to pull away but he dug his nails into her shoulder causing excruciating pain and she went down on her knees. Once on the ground he grabbed her by the hair and hit her in the face. He pushed her the rest of the way to the ground and straddled her. Leah was screaming by now, "Shut Up B#@*!" he said through clenched teeth as he put the knife to her throat and pressed down. She felt it cut so she grabbed his hands and pushed against the force.

"Shut Up B#@*!" he said again, "Or I Will Kill You!" Leah got quiet again but her mind was still racing. Leon reached down and tore off her panties. He was breathing so fast, he reached for his own zipper and got his pants down quickly. He was straddling Leah and making these sick noises. He pinned her legs apart, Leah was still resisting, now she was crying "NO, NO, NO," she was saying. "YES, YES," she heard him say. Now he was trying to penetrate her. In desperation Leah started moving her arms around, squirming so that he could not penetrate her. Her hand touched something, she didn't know what it was and she didn't care. She reached for it again but accidentally pushed it away from her reach. He was still trying to penetrate but Leah was fighting with everything in her.

She began squirming again until she reached the object, it was heavy, a car part of some kind. She found the strength to pick it up, swung with everything in her and hit Leon in the head with the object. Just as she was about to hit him again, he fell limp on top of her. She felt his blood pouring out onto her skin and she began to scream. She pushed him off of her sat up and started screaming. She was sure that he was dead. At that moment she heard someone outside yelling, "Hey, who's in there? Are you alright?" Much to her surprise Leon started to move. Just as the man opened the garage door, he jumped up and bolted past him.

The man let him go and came over to Leah. She was covered in blood. He thought that she was hurt a lot worse than she was but he checked her and found that the majority of the blood was not coming from her. His wife and some of the other neighbors were out by then. "Call the police," he commanded and someone left to do that. "Can you walk?" he asked her and she nodded yes. She wanted to get out of that garage. "Who did this?" she heard someone ask. "One of the guys that lives here," she heard the man say. " Hey that's Gary's sister," someone else said, "They're all over to Ernie's, I'll go get them."

Every one was asking Leah if she were O.K. The police and ambulance had gotten there; they had her on the gurney when most of the people from the party started showing up. Anna, Gary, Michelle and Ernie were the first ones to get there. The police and the ambulance attendants were telling them that she was O.K. and that they were just taking her to the hospital to make sure. "What happened?" Anna was screaming thinking that Cash had done something to her sister. The police said that someone had attacked her and that they knew who it was and was looking for him.

Cash was driving up the street; he was on his way to Anna's when he saw all of the commotion. He saw all of his friends out there so he stopped to see what had happened. He got out of the car and asked. Everyone started talking to him all at once; Cash could not believe what he was hearing. He made his way over to the gurney, looked down at Leah and began to cry. "Oh my God baby, what did I do?" he asked her. "You haven't done anything, this was his sick self," Leah said to him. "Where is he?" Cash wanted to know. "We don't know," the officer said, "He got away before we got here."

The ambulance attendants were telling Cash that they had to leave with Leah but he would not let go of her hand. "We have to go," they said again forcing him to let go of her hand. Cash let go of Leah's hand reluctantly, "I'll be right there," he told her, "I'm coming to the hospital as soon as I can baby," he reassured her as Anna jumped into the ambulance with her sister and they pulled off. Cash stood there in disbelief watching the ambulance take off. He couldn't believe what was happening, he began to cry, at first the tears were silent but after a moment he began to sob. Ernie walked over and put his hand on Cash's shoulder but he pushed it away, stepped a few feet away and began to vomit.

The Security Police had begun their investigation by asking Gary and Ernie questions. Cash came to himself when he heard Gary answer them, "I don't know, but I do know that they have had trouble out of him before." Cash shook his head vigorously in an effort to think straight. The officer asked him if he was O.K. to answer some questions. Cash agreed because he had a lot of questions of his own. He answered all of the questions going all the way back to the first time that he saw Leon following Leah. He became upset all over again as he recalled. He realized that they should have said something to the authorities by now.

The police also shared with them that they were looking for someone who fit Leon's description who had been attempting to stop women in Page Manor by pretending that he was sick. He had recently tried to force one woman out of her car, and another he had tried to force his way into her car. "Don't worry, we'll find him now that we know who he is. He hasn't had time to get very far." The police went back to Leon's brother's house. He'd cooperated fully when he found out what his brother had done. Ernie, Gary, and Cash got into Gary's car and went to the hospital. All of them were quiet during the ride, yet they were all thinking the same thoughts. Make sure that Leah was O.K. and then help the police to find Leon.

When they got to the hospital the police and all their friends from Page Manor were already there. Anna was coming out of the treatment area when Cash got there. She told everyone that Leah was going to be O.K., that there were small cuts and bruises on her neck and face but that she would be O.K. She walked over to Cash and reassured him that things were all right. Anna told him that Leah was asking for him, and that as soon as the police was finished questioning her he could go back and talk to her. Cash sat down and held his head. Partly because he was sad and overwhelmed, but mostly because he felt helpless and embarrassed that this thing had happened to Leah.

He kept his eyes closed because he did not want to look at anyone. People were steadily coming in as they heard what had happened. They were all offering condolences to Anna and Gary and from time to time someone who knew would tell him how sorry they were that this had happened to Leah. Then he heard Michelle's voice, "How is she, is she all right? I finally got the kids down and asked the sitter to stay with them," she reported to Anna. "You didn't tell them what happened did you?" Anna asked her. "No, just that there had been an accident and that everyone was O.K." Michelle told her as her eyes met Cash's.

It was the first time that he had opened up his eyes, he remembered being in this very emergency room the first time that he met Leah. He tried to shake the image from his head but he couldn't. She was so beautiful that day, and so worried about Bianca. "Oh my God Bianca!" he said out loud without realizing it. The thought was too much for him to bear. He stood up realizing how scared she must be right now. He had to talk to Leah right now so while everyone was busy talking he made his way back to the treatment area.

Leah looked up and saw him just as he moved the curtain back. He looked directly into her eyes as he walked past the police to the other side of the cubicle and put his arms around her. They held onto each other for what seemed like an eternity before he took a step back looked in her eyes and asked if she were O.K. The hurt in his eyes was more than Leah could stand and so she pulled him closer, buried her head in his chest and shook her head yes. Cash wanted to make sure that she was O.K. so he pushed her away, looked at her again and asked her again if she were sure she was all right. He touched the bandage on her neck and the bruise on her face. He had to believe now that this was real because here was the evidence. "Did he…?" he asked her without using the words. "No," she said quietly, burying her head back into his chest. Cash wanted her to look at him when she answered just to make sure that she wasn't saying no because of shock or embarrassment, so he pushed her back again and forced her to look at him. She knew him so well that he didn't have to repeat the question, she looked into his eyes and answered him again, "No, he didn't," she said to him again.

Before either of them had a chance to say anything else the police told Cash that they would be charging him with assault with a deadly weapon and "attempted rape." Cash really felt bad because out of all that had happened tonight those words "attempted rape" came as music to his ears. He took a deep breath, let out a deep sigh and held onto Leah as tightly as he could without hurting her. He told her how sorry he was for not being there to protect her.

Leah didn't know what to say. There were so many emotions going on in her head that she was afraid to talk. She held onto Cash as if this would be the last time that she ever saw him. She could not believe that as soon as she made up in her mind to act like an adult and not make a scene that this would happen to her. She began to believe that she was being punished for loving Cash. This had to be her fault. She should have insisted that he go back to his family, or at the very least stopped seeing him.

But she had not been able to find the strength to stay away from him. She'd tried on several occasions but the minute that she saw his face or heard his voice or even thought about him the separation would become to much and she would find herself doing whatever it took to get back together with him. It couldn't be wrong; they loved each other too much. She wasn't being selfish was she? Cash had left his family before they even started seeing each other. "Oh My God," she heard herself say out loud, "Oh My God! Oh My God!" she kept repeating as she began to loosen the grip that she had on Cash and on reality, "Oh My God!"

Cash felt her letting go and tried to hold onto her but she pushed him away. "No, please go away," she told him through the tears that were coming in puddles now. "I can't do this anymore, please go." Cash tried to force her to look at him but she wouldn't, "I am not going to leave you, I can't." "Yes, you have to she told him, GO!" she was yelling at him. "Baby please," Cash was begging her, but the nurse and the police officer were also telling him that he had to leave.

It was one of the hardest things that Cash had ever had to do, but he walked away knowing that Leah was falling apart and that he couldn't do anything to comfort her. As he walked way from the examining room he could still hear her crying. He turned around to go back but someone stopped him. They explained to him that Leah was probably in shock and that he should go away and give her some time with the doctors. Cash heard what they were telling him but he felt something really different from her. Anger rose up in him, as it never had before.

He walked back into the waiting room; the anger was more than he could even comprehend. How could this happen? Could this be his fault? Leah never would have left the party if it weren't for him. She never would have left walking by her self. How could he not have known how dangerous Leon was? Why hadn't he left her alone? Michelle and Anna had nearly begged him to stop seeing her. Why hadn't he listened? He looked around the waiting room and saw everyone looking at him. Anna looked as if she felt sorry for him but Michelle looked as if she hated his guts.

All of the thoughts and emotions that were flooding his mind were becoming too much to bear. He just wanted it all to stop. Gary seemed to understand exactly what he was going through. He walked over to him and put his hand on his shoulder. "Man, you're going to be O.K., Leah's going to be O.K., we all are we're going to get through this." Cash let the tears come that he had been holding back, all of the anger and the hurt came flooding out. This night was supposed to end so differently, finally Leah understood that he loved and had chosen her.

All of the drama that he'd had to go through with Carla that night in an effort to get back to Leah. He'd finally been completely honest with her telling her that he'd decided that he was going to be with Leah. She'd cried, begged and pleaded with him not to leave her and the kids. He'd made her a promise that he wouldn't do anything right away, that he would always take care of his children and make sure that she was O.K. He knew that she was hurt but felt peaceful about the decision that he'd made. Then he got in his car to find Leah and tell her about his decision, only to find out that she had nearly been killed.

Nearly killed by someone who he now felt he should have turned into the police months ago. His thoughts went back to all of the times that Leon had harassed them. Why hadn't he taken this man seriously? The anger returned with a vengeance. Now Ernie was standing with him. His two closest friends were trying to console him but could not find the words. Cash's anger continued to grow. "Man this sh*@ is crazy," he finally said, he said through the tears, "This is not right, she don't deserve this." Ernie knew where this was headed; he knew that his friend was feeling guilty about what happened to Leah. He was trying to console him but he would not be consoled. "Man this is on me," Cash finally said, "This is on me." "You damned right it's on you," he heard Michelle say. Cash looked at her to find that same look of contempt that she'd had for him lately multiplied ten times over.

"Stop it Michelle," Anna told her, "This is not his fault, this is not anybody's fault but that freak's who did this to her." Gary and Ernie echoed what Anna was saying. Cash walked outside, he had to move, the pain was too much for him to stand still. It was so heart wrenching that it had become physical, a scream rose up from within him that even he didn't recognize. Gary and Ernie followed him outside. "I can't take this man," he told them, "This hurts too much man I got to go." "Hold on man, we're coming with you," Gary told him. He didn't trust Cash to be alone right now.

Gary went back into the emergency room and told Anna that he and Ernie were leaving with Cash. Anna begged him not to do or let Cash do anything crazy. The minute that they were gone Anna began to pray. She prayed that God would bring Leah through this. She prayed for Cash and for Carla, and then oddly enough she began to pray for Leon. She prayed that either he would be long gone or that the police would find him fast before the men of Page Manor could. Those men being her husband Gary, Ernie, who she still cared about, and Cash who her sister loved more than she understood. She was right to pray, but her prayer concerning Leon would fall on deaf ears.

The men headed back toward Page Manor. Ernie suggested they go back to his house for a drink. Gary agreed, Cash didn't say anything and they took that as yes. All during the ride home he was quiet. His friends had assured him that this wasn't his fault and that Leah would not blame him for what happened. But they had not seen the way she'd acted. They didn't hear her ask him to leave. It kept playing over and over in his mind. He wanted it to stop; he wanted to turn off the thoughts that were going through his head so he didn't object when Ernie suggested a drink.

Ernie and Gary tried to make small talk about what was going on but Cash just looked out of the window as they drove through Page Manor. It was while he was looking out of the window that he saw the shadow pass between the buildings. He jumped as if someone had shocked him, "Hey," was all that he could get out. "What's up?" Gary asked him. "I'm not sure man, turn around and go back," Cash told him.

Gary turned the car around quickly and they headed back the other way. This time, Ernie saw him before Cash and Gary. "There he is, it's Leon!" Ernie said. He didn't have to say anything else. Gary pulled the car over and all three men jumped out. Leon saw them and began to run. Even though he was hurt and still bleeding from being hit in the head by Leah he was running for his life. Gary was not a runner but kept them in his sights, Ernie and Cash however were athletes and closed the gap between them and Leon pretty quickly. But it would be Cash that would actually reach out and grab him, slowing him up just enough for Ernie to tackle him.

The three of them rolled onto the ground together. Ernie somehow landed on Leon's knee and got the wind knocked out of him. Cash got up immediately and began to punch and kick Leon. He tried at first to fight back but all of the frustration and anger that Cash had been feeling was being channeled into every blow, every kick brought a kind of twisted satisfaction to Cash. It was only for a few minutes but by the time Gary made it to where they were and Ernie caught his breath, Cash had beaten Leon up pretty bad. They had to pull him off and beg him to stop kicking and hitting him. While they were holding Cash Leon tried to stagger to his feet and run but Gary grabbed him and began dragging him toward the street.

Neighbors began to come out and the men asked them to call Security Police and they did. It wasn't long before they got there to arrest Leon, but they also had some questions for them regarding Leon's injuries. The neighbors reported to the police that Leon had kept fighting and trying to leave the scene and that the men were simply trying to keep him there until the police arrived. The police took the report and Leon and left.

Cash sat on the curb and wept. He had just nearly taken a man's life. He'd never considered himself a violent man but he knew that if Ernie and Gary were not there he could have and probably would have killed him. What really scared him was the satisfaction that he had felt with every blow; it felt good to pay him back for what he'd done to Leah, for how he'd turned all of their lives upside down. Now at least he could rest in the fact that he would not be getting away with it.

CHAPTER TWENTY-FIVE

The next few weeks were crazy for every body. Cash and Leah thought that the worst was behind them but that would not turn out to be the truth. A few days after the police had arrested Leon, Cash had been called into the office of his Colonel. Colonel Green had gotten most of the details of what happened and wanted Cash to fill in the blanks. Once he began to say what happened the Colonel began to question him about his relationship with Leah. Cash could not lie to the Colonel and it would not have done him any good any way because he'd gotten all of the details from Carla.

Carla had decided that even though she felt sorry about what happened to Leah, she still wanted her husband back and was willing to pull out all of the stops to make that happen. She'd gone to the Colonel and told him everything including the fact that Cash for the most part had moved out of the unit and was having an out in the open affair with Leah. The end result was that Cash was told that either he move back into the unit with his family, or give it up and allow them to go back to Pennsylvania. He was also told that the Air Force frowned on infidelity and that he had to be careful what he did in public. The Colonel stopped just short of telling him that he would have to stop seeing Leah. It was a devastating blow on top of everything else that was going on.

Leah was determined not to let what happened to her stop her from living a normal life, but when she got the news that Cash had to move back in with Carla it was almost more than she could stand. She'd made a decision not to see him anymore but of course that wouldn't last very long. She missed him too much. Not only that but Leah started to feel ostracized. It felt as if people thought that she'd gotten what she deserved for having an affair with Cash. She'd never felt so lonely in her life. Leah's life now centered around going to school and coming home period. She didn't hang out anymore and rarely saw any of her friends. She was beginning to drink more than ever.

Gary and Anna were scheduled to take a vacation, which meant she would be alone in the unit with Bianca. The first night they were gone Leah snuggled up close to Bianca and cried herself to sleep. When they got up the next morning she realized that things were not as bad as they had appeared lately. For the first time in a long time she was able to take a deep breath and believe that she really could go on with her life. She knew it would be hard but she also knew that for the Bianca's sake if nothing else she had to go on. There was a carnival going on across the street and she decided that she and Bianca would go and spend some quality time together. She was going through her morning motions when the phone rang. She expected it to be Anna even though she'd talked to her last night and assured her that she and Bianca were fine. But, it wasn't Anna it was Ernie. He'd called to check on Leah and the baby because he knew that Anna and Gary were out of town.

"It is so sweet of you to call," Leah told him happy to hear a friendly voice. "I would have called before now but we all thought we should give you some time" Ernie told her, "What you up to around there?" Leah told him that she was going to take Bianca to the carnival today and just hang out. "It's good to see you getting back out, we've missed seeing you around," Ernie told her. "Yeah, I've missed you all too, tell Sheila that I said thanks for her prayers and tell Michelle that I will call her later." Leah told him anxious to hang up. Ernie made her promise that she would call if they needed anything and they hung up.

Leah continued with her morning ritual, it seemed a lot easier this morning. She took great care and pride in the way she dressed herself and the baby. She wanted to let the world know that she wasn't about to just lie down and die. She'd convinced herself that life was worth living with or without Cash and she was going to do just that, LIVE! She turned on some music and began to dance around and laugh with Bianca. It had been a long time since she'd truly laughed or saw Bianca laugh for that matter. She opened the blinds and the front door careful to lock the screen. This in itself was a great victory for her because she'd spent all of her mornings in the dark lately.

She began to realize that her true friends still loved her. She convinced herself that everybody that she needed to be in her life was still going to be there for her. She'd convinced herself for the moment that she didn't need Cash in her life no matter how bad she wanted him. She began to remember how she thought that she would not be able to live without Jamie, how she'd found out that she could not only live without him but she and Bianca had begun to have a better life without him, that was up until now. That one thought brought her mood crashing down. Instantly her thoughts turned to how much she missed Cash. She brought Bianca into the den, sat down and played with her for a while and was soon laughing again. Bianca had a way of making her laugh when no one else could.

Leah didn't know that she and Bianca were being watched. She felt safe for the first time in a long time. She had no idea that Cash had approached the door and was watching them interact. Just watching her made him happier than he'd been in a very long time. She'd told him that under the circumstances she did not want to see him anymore. He thought that it was like before, she'd be mad for a few days, she'd start missing him and give in. But it wasn't like that at all this time. She'd been able to stick to her guns and not see him anymore. He was sure that Anna and Michelle were encouraging her. Now he'd heard from Ernie that Gary and Anna were out of town and he had to try to see her.

Cash had called her a few times to 'check on her' or so he'd said. Each time before the call ended he would tell her how much he missed her and Bianca and try to get Leah to agree to see him. Each time she'd thanked him for calling to check on them, and said that she would not see him. His heart ached for her; as he stood there watching her and Bianca, he was both happy and sad at the same time. He was happy that they were smiling and laughing again, but it made him sad to see that they could be happy without him. He stood there at the door for a few minutes just watching them.

Leah continued playing with Bianca but no matter how much she tried not to think about Cash, this morning it wasn't working. She decided to do the only thing that she knew would ease the pain, take a drink. She set Bianca up with snacks and turned on Barney. She went around the back of the unit to the kitchen, poured herself a stiff drink and drank it down. She rinsed her mouth, went to her purse for a breath mint, the purse slipped from her hand. When she stood up from the purse she saw Cash standing at the door.

Her heart stopped beating for a moment and she realized that she wasn't breathing. They stood there looking at each other for a minute. "God, he looks good" she thought to herself. "Are you going to open the door or not?" he finally questioned her. Leah hesitated for a minute and Cash spoke again, "I just want to see for myself that you're alright." It made sense, everybody knew that Anna and Gary were out of town, everyone had been "calling or stopping by to make sure they were O.K.." She went to the door and unlocked it. Cash stepped inside the door, when he turned around to lock it Leah walked into the den and picked up Bianca.

Cash took a deep breath, her reaction to him hurt, a lot. They hadn't seen each other in weeks and it was obvious that she was uncomfortable being alone with him. He walked into the den, the minute that Bianca saw him she jumped from her mother's arms and ran into his. He picked her up and held her close. Leah could tell that he'd missed her and that she'd missed him. She immediately began to talk to him about the carnival they were going to. She was sure that Cash was there to take them. Cash took another deep breath trying his best not to let Bianca see how much what she was saying was hurting him. He looked at Leah and noticed that it was hurting her just as much to hear Bianca talk about the three of them being together. Cash hugged her tight, kissed her on her cheek and said, "sounds like you and Mommy were planning a girls afternoon out, let me see if I can change her mind." "Yaah!" Bianca said as she jumped down and ran to the T.V.

"So, you guys are going to the carnival," Cash said trying to make small talk. "Yes, we are," Leah told him irritated that being this close to him made her so uncomfortable. Cash tried to touch her but she stood and walked away. God his heart couldn't take her rejecting him. He began to wonder if she knew that he was back with his wife in every way. Leah walked into the living area and sat down. Cash waited a few seconds and followed her into the other room. "You shouldn't be here," she told him. "You're right and neither should you, we should be someplace together right now," Cash told her. "You should be right where you are, with your wife and kids," Leah told him, something like panic was rising up in her and she couldn't stop it.

"Please baby don't." Cash barely got the words out of his mouth before Leah tore into him. "Don't what Cash? Don't say it out loud? As if that somehow is going to make it any less the truth." Cash walked toward her desperate to put his arms around her, to comfort her but that was the last thing she wanted to happen. She knew that if she let him touch her it would be over, she would not be able to stop herself from falling into his arms and back under his spell. Every time that he tried t o touch her she would move away. "It was a choice that I was forced to make, for my kids," he thought that telling her this would make things better but the statement only made things worse.

"So you made it, what do you want from me?" Leah was angry and hurt, "It was bad enough the way things were just knowing that you were still married to her, now you want me to accept the fact that the two of you are living under the same roof as husband and wife? Now you want me to really be the other woman. Well I'm tired of that role, you're going to have to find someone else to play that part for you. Please leave!" Cash stood there as if someone had just stabbed him but he didn't move. "I'm not going to leave you like this," he finally said as calmly as he could.

He was really scared. For the first time since he'd met Leah she appeared to be in control. Even though she was angry and obviously hurt she appeared to know what was best for her. Not only that but it also appeared that she was willing to go through whatever she had to, to get it. Cash was thinking fast, they'd fought before, she'd been really mad at him before. Then he remembered; all those times before when she was so angry with him all he'd had to do was get his arms around her and hold her until she gave in. His confidence was coming back. He walked toward Leah. She saw the look on his face and began to back away.

"No Cash, not this time," Leah told him as she backed away, "Please go!" Cash wasn't listening to the words she was saying. He was watching her eyes and seeing the desperation that was in them. He could see that she was desperate, but not for him to leave. He got that she was angry and hurt, he knew that she felt alone and abandoned by him. He knew that she felt ostracized by the Air Force community he understood all of that. His mind told him that the best thing to do would be to leave her alone and let her continue to heal. But his heart was telling him that she needed to be held, that if they could just spend some time together the way they used to everything would be all right.

"You know that I'm not going to do that," he told her continuing to walk toward her, "You are going to have to convince me that's what you really want, and you can't do that while you're running from me." Leah sat down and began to cry. Cash knew that he'd won this round. He walked over and sat next to her, "I love you, and I don't know what's going to happen to us. All I know is that I won't let it end like this, not with you hating me. If you don't want to be with me anymore I understand that, but let me help you get through this," Cash put his hand on her shoulder, he was afraid to really touch her, to put his arms around her and hold her the way he wanted to.

The minute he touched her he felt her body give in. It wasn't the sexual kind of surrender that he'd experienced with her time and again when they fought, but instead it was the kind of surrender that gave him permission to comfort her. Leah allowed the tears to flow, something that she hadn't been able to do since all of this began to happen to her. Each time that she had began to cry she'd reminded herself that she had to be strong, that crying meant that she was weak, and she had to be strong not only to save face for herself but to be strong for Bianca as well. For the first time since this ordeal began she felt as if she didn't have to hide her pain. Cash put his arms around her and held her while she wept quietly.

All of the pain that she'd felt all lately came flooding to the surface at that moment. She had wanted to break down and cry so many times lately, but now while Cash held her she allowed herself to cry. Cash didn't talk; he didn't even know what to say he just held her for the next few minutes while she cried. Before he knew it he was sharing her tears. He knew that a lot of what she was going through was his fault. He couldn't help but to feel her pain. He also began to cry. He kept apologizing over and over. When Leah had no more tears to cry she got up and walked into the restroom, washed her face and checked on Bianca. Bianca had fallen asleep with the very first toy that Cash had given her. She was so peaceful, how could she disturb her peace again by not allowing Cash to continue to be a part of her life?

Leah didn't know how she was going to deal with what was happening between them. She knew how much she missed Cash and she could only imagine how much her baby girl missed him. She'd begun to ask about him all of the time and Leah was tired of making excuses. Just then Cash walked out of the bathroom, picked Bianca up and held her close for a few minutes before he laid her in the playpen. He sat down on the couch and held his head in his hands. He couldn't believe how screwed up things had become and how much of it was his fault. He took a few deep breaths and looked back up at Leah who for the first time realized that he was going through his own personal torture because of the situation.

Leah sat next to him and he reached for her hand. They both inhaled almost simultaneously and it brought a smile to their faces. They assured each other that things were going to be O.K. but nothing could have been further from the truth, at least as far as their relationship was concerned. Even while they were reassuring each other they both knew things were changing between them, but neither of them wanted to let go. Cash left to go back to work and Leah took Bianca to the carnival and all would be well, at least for a while.

CHAPTER TWENTY-SIX

Cash and Leah had been seeing each other on a regular basis again. Not out in the open as they had before, they'd learned to be discreet meeting at James' house some nights and spend time together during the day at Leah's. Lately Cash seemed to have become more distant and she was planning to ask him about it. It was his birthday, Halloween night. They'd run into each other as Leah and Bianca were coming out of the house. Cash asked her why Bianca didn't have on a jacket and instructed her to go back and get one for her. Leah sent her nieces and nephew ahead and went back for the jacket. When she came back outside Cash and his children were long gone.

Leah wasn't concerned, she figured that she would see him later and they would spend at least part of his birthday together. She caught up with the kids, put Bianca's jacket on and went ahead with the Halloween fun. It wasn't until later on that night that things would begin to go bad for her. She expected Cash to call but when he didn't she decided to walk up to the Joint to find out if he was there. When she got to the parking lot she spotted Cash's car, figuring that she had gotten her signals crossed she went into the bar expecting to find Cash and his friends partying. The club was packed and it was hard for her to see where he was. Leah sat down and ordered a drink, she'd just about come to the conclusion that Cash wasn't there when she spotted his friend Willie.

Willie was fine!!! When people saw him and Cash together they assumed they were brothers but Willie was even more handsome than Cash. Willie spotted her as well and began to make his way through the crowd to the table where Leah sat. Leah smiled as she watched him walk her way. He was confident and sexy and most of all, he was single. He finally made it to the table, hugged Leah and sat down. "Hey, what's going on?" he asked seeming a little confused. "Nothing much," Leah answered, "What's going on with you?" Willie had a very confused look on his face. "Did your boy leave you here by yourself?" Without knowing it Willie had just answered Leah's question regarding where Cash was. "No, I just got here," she was able to pull off acting as if it didn't matter that Cash had obviously been there and left. Willie and Leah made small talk but questions were burning in Leah's mind, where was Cash and whom was he spending his birthday with?

Willie made it obvious that he was interested in more than just having a drink and a conversation with her. Leah was flattered but in her mind she could never be low down enough to get involved with one of Cash's friends. Willie was upset with her because of her loyalty to Cash, if she only knew that Cash had just left the club with another woman, that wasn't his wife maybe she wouldn't be so loyal. He decided against telling her but promised her that he'd see her around and left the table. Leah was confused again, not only by the fact that Cash seemed to have disappeared, but also with Willie's behavior. She shook her head and decided that she wasn't going to sit here waiting for Cash.

She got up and walked to the door, looked down the outside corridor that led to the parking lot and walked out. When she got to the parking lot she saw that Cash's car was still there and decided to leave him a note. She went back into the bar, got a pen and a napkin and wrote, " You're not with me and you're not at home, where are you and who are you with?" She went back outside and placed the note on the windshield. She didn't feel comfortable walking home so went back into the bar and asked Willie for a ride home. He agreed and they left for the short ride to Leah's house.

Willie was quiet until they pulled up in front of Leah's house. He apologized to her for getting angry at the club explaining that he just didn't understand the attraction and the loyalty she felt for Cash. He wanted to tell her so badly that Cash was with someone else as they spoke but he didn't want to hurt her. Leah acknowledged to Willie that she was feeling a lot of confusion where Cash was concerned and knew with a certainty that their relationship was changing. She assured him that her eyes were wide open and that she would make sure things turned out to her advantage.

Leah thanked Willie for his concern, got out of the car and went into the house. The best way to describe what she was feeling was numb. She went out back and smoked a joint, came back inside and poured a drink. She turned on some music and started to dance alone. The Commodores were singing "Easy" which was one of Cash's favorites when the phone rang.

Leah expected it to be Cash telling her that he was on his way to pick her up but instead it was Carla, Cash's wife. "I would appreciate it if you would not leave notes on my husband's car, it is not any of your business where he is or who he's with," Carla said apparently irritated. Leah was shocked to say the least but her reply was quick, cruel and it cut deep, " Sweetie, don't get mad at me because you can't find your husband, again. I'll do you a favor though, when he gets here I'll tell him you're looking for him."

Leah was in awe at how cruel she'd been to Carla and even more than that how good it felt. The numbness that she'd been feeling was slowly being replaced with a coldness that wasn't familiar to Leah. She thought the coldness was a new form of an old pain but this wasn't painful. She laughed to herself at the thought of how angry she'd made Carla; even more satisfying to her was the thought of how Cash would have to answer to her. Leah poured herself another drink and settled in for the evening. She'd already made up her mind that if and when Cash called she would not be spending any time with him. She was tired of all of the drama and although she still didn't think that she'd ever consider going out with Willie, the image of him burned in her mind enough to allow her to see for the first time that there were other men interested in her, and it was time for her to explore other options. As of this moment her loyalty to Cash Windsor was over.

Leah was convinced that she was through with Cash. She wasn't sure how things were going to play out, but she knew it was over. She was deep in her thoughts when the phone rang again. The sound of the phone shook her loose from her thoughts. A devious smile came across her face; she thought that it would be Carla calling again. She took a deep breath and answered the phone. "Hey, what's up?" it was Cash, "I'm sorry I meant to call you before now but I was hanging out with some friends and time just got away from me; I'm on my way there now," Cash was smooth and it caused Leah to wonder about all of the times she'd just accepted his excuses without question. She laughed to herself.

"No, I think you'd better go and see about your wife, she's looking for you," Leah was oozing sarcasm and coldness. "What do you mean she's looking for me?" Cash asked. "Just what I said, she's looking for you," Leah was so calm that Cash didn't know what to make of the situation, but he knew that it wasn't good. "How do you know she's looking for me?" he asked her. "I went to the Joint looking for you and you weren't there, I left a note on your car and she called to remind me that it wasn't any of my business where you were," Leah came clean quickly, something that she would never have done in the past. "You did what?" Cash was furious. Cash's reaction let Leah know that she was right to let go. She shook her head as the reality of the situation became crystal clear, "Go see about your wife," she said to him.

Cash didn't know what to think, Leah was so different. He didn't know what to make of this new attitude that she had. He took a deep breath and told her he'd talk to her in the morning. She told him that was fine but even the way she said it worried Cash. Cash did just what he said; he went home to see about his wife who was furious with him. This was also a new situation for him because he had not cared what she thought for quite some time. Now he was desperate for her to believe that he wasn't with Leah tonight, that they hadn't been together lately, all of which was the truth. To calm her down and to seal the deal Cash made love to his wife that night and in his heart he knew this was the end of Leah and him.

The next morning Leah was getting ready for school. She'd spent the night thinking about her relationship with Cash and what he might be facing at home with his wife. She knew they were fighting and she wasn't sorry. In her mind they were both getting what they deserved. Leah was feeling better about herself than she had in a long time. She took extra care in grooming herself this morning. She'd made up her mind that she would start accepting some of the attentions that the guys were paying her lately. No longer would she sit around waiting for Cash to make himself available that was over. Cash had not called at the crack of dawn as he usually did when they fought which said a lot to Leah.

Just as she was about to go out the door Cash called. She knew that it was him when the phone rang. She started not to answer it but changed her mind. "Hello," she said prepared for the fall out from last night. "Hey," was all he could manage to say at first. "Hey yourself," she said quickly, "What's up?" Cash was trying his best to feel her out this morning. "What do you mean what's up, why did you do that?" he asked. "Do what?" she answered. "You know what I'm talking about, what did the note say?" Leah told him exactly what she'd written in a matter-of-fact way, "It said, you're not at home and you're not with me, where are you and who are you with?" "I wish that you hadn't done that," Cash told her. "But I did, so now what?" Leah was still being cold.

"We need to talk, I'm not sure that I'll be able to get away tonight but if I can I'll call you," Cash told her this knowing that he'd already made plans for the night. "Fine," Leah told him making up in her mind that she wasn't going to see him tonight or any time soon. She hung up the phone, took Bianca to daycare and went to school. She was so different that day that it was noticeable to nearly everyone she knew. Her friend Sara told her at lunch, "I can almost see the old you coming back." Leah agreed and they made a date to go to the Westside Club that night.

Leah went home full of energy that day, she asked Anna and Gary if she could use their van to go out in that night and they agreed. They too were happy to see her getting back to her old self. Gary told her she could use the van if she picked up her nephew from his soccer practice and she agreed. When she picked up her nephew he had soccer and baseball equipment with him. He laid it on the floor of the van and she took him home. Leah got dressed quickly, she was determined to get to Sara's before Cash called and messed up her plans. In her mind, if she left before he called she wouldn't have to play games, lie, or make excuses as to why she wouldn't see him. Once she left Page Manor she felt that she was home free, she got to Sara's, had a few drinks and a few laughs and left for the club.

Leah was as excited to be going out, and for the first time in a long time she felt free. For a moment she reflected on how young she was and how much she'd already been through and she was determined to get through at least this night without worrying about what Cash would say. They were busy talking and laughing when she pulled into the parking lot of the club. Sara was so busy talking and laughing that she didn't notice that Leah had stopped talking. As soon as she drove into the lot she'd spotted Cash's car. Knowing that there was at least one other car like it she drove around to the spot where the car was parked. She pulled up behind the car to make sure that it was his and it was.

She wasn't quite sure what to feel at that point because Cash was supposed to be at home, and he wasn't at home then he was supposed to have called her so that they could talk. But instead, here he was at the club. Sara watched her friends mood change drastically, "Come on girl, we came to have some fun, forget him," she tried to calm the situation as she saw her friend getting angry. "Well maybe it's Carla," Leah tried to reason not believing in a million years that Cash would cross her this way. There was a parking space right next to the car and Leah parked there reasoning that if by chance she missed him in the club he would know that she knew he was there.

She shook herself and started talking and laughing with Sara as they walked into the club. This was becoming repetitious; there she was again scanning the crowd looking for Cash. It was early on a Thursday night but there was a decent crowd and it took her a minute to spot him. When she did she could not believe what she saw, in one section of the club there were tall tables with bar stools for seats. These tables were for the lovers in the house because each table only had two seats. Cash was not sitting in the seat but he was leaning on the table and smiling that million dollar, sexy smile while gazing into the eyes of a woman who looked a lot like Leah. Leah took in the whole scenario, Cash had not seen her and her mind was racing to explore her options.

Sara followed Leah's gaze and finally spotted Cash and the woman as well. "Oh s#@!" was all that she could manage to say. In an instant her mind was flooded with ideas as to how to handle the situation, one more devious than the next. Just as she had decided to calmly approach the cute couple and introduce herself, Cash looked up from his conversation and spotted her. For an instant their eyes locked and she could read his lips as he mouthed the word "damn." Cash stood up straight like a deer caught in someone's headlights as Leah took a few steps toward him and the young lady.

As Leah began to walk toward them all of a sudden something broke through all of the anger and coldness. Leah did not have to try to figure this one out she knew this feeling very well. It was strangely different though in that it seemed it was magnified one hundred times over. It literally felt as if someone had just stabbed her and it stopped her dead in her tracks. Cash had braced himself for her to approach; when she started toward him their eyes were locked. He was trying to prepare for what she might do or say when she got to him when he saw her stop.

The pain and humiliation that she was feeling was more than she could bear. She couldn't even meet his gaze anymore. She turned around and headed for the door. She heard him calling her name but she kept going. She heard Sara saying something about it being all right but she kept going. The pain seemed physical; she had to get out of there. She pushed through the crowd and made her way out the door. As soon as she got outside she went around the side of the building so that Cash would not be able to find her. She made it just in time before she heard him asking Sara where she had gone. Sara told him, "Where ever she is I hope that you never find her." "Sara I know you mad at me and I don't blame you, but this is between Leah and me, come on you saw her, I'm scared that she won't be able to handle this," Cash was pleading now. "Then you shouldn't have done it, if I did know where she was I wouldn't tell you."

Leah started walking; she just wanted to get to the van so that she could leave. The pain was too much, by the time that she made it to the van she was bent over with the pain. There was no doubt it was physical now. She began to vomit and was very near passing out. She opened the side door of the van to sit inside so that she could get herself together. She was trying to collect herself but the pain was too much. She looked over and saw his car and it made her stomach hurt worse, she leaned inside of the van and closed her eyes tight. She wanted this all to be a bad dream, she wanted the pain to go away but it wouldn't. She opened her eyes and saw her nephews bat lying on the floor of the van.

The thought immediately came to her mind to break the window but she told herself not to do it. She was literally shaking her head no when she heard him say her name. "Leah, baby please," he was saying as he was walking toward her. "Oh no, you are not about to touch me," she was saying more to herself than to him. "Baby we was just talking, just talking," she heard him say. Now on top of everything else he was trying to lie to her, to play on her intelligence. Leah picked up the bat. When Cash saw her with the bat he hesitated but only for a minute.

He started walking toward her again, "Baby we need to talk." "Talk about what Cash? About what a liar you are?" she swung the bat and it shattered the back passenger window. Leah was more surprised than he was but it made the pain ease up so she swung the bat again, this time she hit the body of the car. "Baby please don't do this," Cash pleaded with her. A crowd was gathering by now but neither of them cared. "Don't do what Cash? Don't make a scene, don't hurt your precious car, what is it that you don't want me to do?" she swung the bat again and broke the mirror from the side of the car. "Baby please, don't do this" Cash said and somehow either his words or his tone was able to penetrate the hurt and anger.

Leah dropped the bat and fell to the ground herself. She began to cry.

Cash moved the bat and got down on the ground with her and held her. He was genuinely sorry that he'd hurt her. Sara was telling Leah that someone had called the police and they should leave but Leah couldn't move. Cash was apologizing over and over again, something that he'd been doing a lot of lately. Leah made it to her feet. Cash stood up as well. Leah looked at what she'd done, "I'm sorry about your car," she managed to say. Cash was holding her hand, "I'm not worried about the car, we need to talk." "We don't have anything to talk about Cash, I don't want to hear anything that you have to say," she said more calm now than she'd been since the day she met him. "Baby please," Cash was saying holding on to her hand as she was walking away. "I can't do this anymore Cash, I'm sorry about your car I will pay for it."

Just as Cash let go of her hand the police pulled up. Leah knew she was going to jail but it didn't matter. This part of her life was over and whatever she had to do to be sure of it she would do even if it meant her going to jail. The policeman stepped out of the car took a look at the situation and said, "Whoa, anybody care to tell me what's going on here?" Leah was just about to make a confession when Cash came up behind her and put his arms around her. "It's just a misunderstanding officer everything is O.K." Leah turned around and looked at him. Cash looked first at the officer and then back at Leah, "It's just a misunderstanding, the young lady was just about to leave and go home to see about her daughter." Leah understood what Cash was trying to do but she was still very angry with him. "Whose car is this?" the officer asked, "and who did this?" Cash wasn't about to let her go to jail on top of everything else, "It's my car officer, and it doesn't matter who did it, I'll take care of it," he said more to Leah than to the officer.

The officer informed them that they had to leave the area or risk being arrested. Leah broke Cash's hold on her and got into her sister's van. Cash was still trying to justify what she'd just seen but she wasn't hearing it. Once Sara was in the van Leah pulled off leaving him standing there trying to explain. Leah had never felt so betrayed in her life, she had flashes of what she'd gone through with Jamie and Tammie, but that pain seemed minute compared to this. She just began to drive. Sara must have asked if she were O.K. four or five times before she got a response, "I will be," Leah said more cold than her friend had ever heard and Sara was immediately afraid for her friend.

Leah drove back to Sara's house. Once in Sara's driveway she broke down and cried. How could she be so stupid, again? How could she have trusted him even after he'd gone back to his wife? When was this pain in her life ever going to stop? When were the men that she loved and trusted, the ones that were supposed to be protecting her going to stop hurting her? What was it going to take? The pain was unbearable; she got physically sick so she stepped out of the van to throw up. Sara went into the house to get her something to drink.

Leah took the cold drink and leaned against the van. She assured Sara that she would be all right and was about to leave when Cash pulled up. "This brother got way too many nerves for me," now Sara was irritated. Leah handed Sara the glass and got into the truck. She was trying to pull off but Cash jumped up on the footstool and held onto the steering wheel. "Stop it Leah, we need to talk," Cash was desperate to talk to her. Leah still had her foot on the gas and the car was moving slowly.

Cash reached across and grabbed the steering wheel on the other side, which placed his forearm across Leah's neck. "Stop the damn van, now!" he yelled. Leah stopped the van; the last thing that she wanted was to fight with him. She just wanted to go home. Cash jammed the gearshift into park and took the keys out of the ignition. He stepped down from the footstool and opened the van door. Sara was yelling at Cash to leave her alone and let her leave. Cash told her to mind her own business and reached for Leah's hand to help her from the van. Leah just sat there so Cash took her by the arm and pulled her as gently as he could from the van.

Leah leaned arms folded across her chest up against the van. She just didn't want to hear anything he had to say. Cash put his arms around her anyway. There was no triumph this time sexual or otherwise. There was no desire in her at all, no longing, no trust. She just stood there arms folded, sad and broken. "I never meant for things to go this way Leah, I never meant to hurt you," Cash told her. "It doesn't make any difference, it's done, I just want to go home" Leah told him.

Cash wanted to look into her eyes but she wouldn't look at him. She just stood there shaking her head. "Please baby, talk to me," Cash was pleading with her now. Leah was so angry with him; she finally looked up at him, "And say what Cash? That I understand, that it's O.K., well I don't understand and it is definitely not O.K. You are so full of shit, you could have let me go a long time ago but no, for whatever your sick twisted reasons are you just want to hold on. But I'm not blaming all of this on you because I wanted to hold on too, but I don't anymore. I'm tired, I don't want to do this anymore, and I won't do this anymore. Go home to your wife and let her put up with your bullsh*@, I'm done."

Cash didn't let go, he just held onto her, "You don't mean this," he finally said. "Oh, yes I do" Leah said trying to push him away. He was angry now; he got a tighter grip on her and pushed her back up against the van. He grabbed her by her hair and forced her head back, all of the memories of Leon came flooding back to her mind. Her body went numb. "This is not over," he said right before he forced her to kiss him. Leah had never seen him this angry before. She wasn't sure what he would do next so she stopped fighting him.

The minute that he stopped kissing her she asked for her keys. He stood there for a minute not believing what was happening. In that moment he realized she meant what she said, at least for the moment. He stepped away from her and handed her the keys. Leah took them, stepped into the van and started it. She looked straight ahead as she put the car into gear. Cash just stood there watching, "This is not over," she heard him say over the engine. She turned and looked him square in the eye and said "STAY AWAY FROM ME," she told him as she pulled off.

CHAPTER TWENTY-SEVEN

The next few weeks were crazy. Cash refused to accept that things were over between he and Leah. Everywhere she went he showed up begging her to take him back. She continued to stand her ground. She wanted nothing to do with him. Now all of their friends were trying to keep Cash away from Leah. He and Uncle Ernie had gotten close to a fistfight because he wouldn't stay away. Anna and Gary had barred him from their unit, but it didn't matter. The minute he knew they were gone he would show up.

Leah was getting ready for school. She'd gotten her nieces and nephew off to school and dropped the toddlers off at Michelle's. She had been fighting to stay away from Cash for weeks and it was beginning to get to her. Her mind told her this was the right thing to do, but her heart and her body were beginning to ache from missing him. Every time she closed her eyes she could feel him, smell him, even taste him. She couldn't go back, she had to stay away from him. She knew this aching would go away, it had with Jamie but Cash was part of the reason for that. She sat down on the couch and began to cry.

She heard the door open and assumed that it was her sister or brother-in-law coming home to check on her. She wiped her eyes and stood up but when she turned around it was Cash standing in the living room. Everything in her went limp and she sat back down on the couch. She was so tired of fighting him, especially since she missed him so much. Cash walked over and sat next to her on the couch. He didn't touch her he just kept saying, "I can't do this, I need you." She couldn't fight him anymore; she laid her head on his shoulders and cried.

He put his arms around her and held her, took some deep breaths and started to cry too. They spent the morning together consoling each other the only way they knew how. Before they knew it the entire morning was gone. It wouldn't be long before someone would be looking for one or both of them. "Let's get out of here," he told her, "Throw something in a bag and let's go to Cincinnati." Leah didn't have to be told twice, she went upstairs, pulled out a suitcase and began to pack some underwear. She realized that she didn't know how long they would be gone so she started back down the stairs to ask him about clothes and Bianca.

She heard him talking to someone and assumed that he was on the phone. She was frozen when she heard him saying that he was going to Cincinnati to pick up recruits and that he would be back tomorrow. That would have been O.K., but what wasn't O.K. was hearing him say "I will be back in time to pack for us to go to Tennessee, tell the kids I'll see them tomorrow night, and I Love you." Just as he was hanging up the phone, he saw Leah on the stairs. He didn't know how much she'd heard but it didn't take long for her eyes to tell him.

"Baby," he said with this pleading look on his face. "No Cash, just go," she told him. "Listen, I didn't know that we were going to get back together today" he tried to lie his way out. "So instead of telling her that we're back together you plan a trip with her for when we come back?" she asked him, "No, why don't you just go to Tennessee and I'll see you when you get back," Leah was lying through her teeth. "I know that you are just saying that but I will see you when I get back" Cash told her. "Of course you will" Leah said knowing that if he did he would not like what he saw.

After Cash left the unit Leah sat there trying to process what had just happened, again. She could not deny that her body was more satisfied than it probably had ever been. Cash was a great lover if nothing else. She wasn't sad and she didn't feel stupid as she usually did. This time she knew why she had given in to him. It was sex, pure and simple. She realized that it wasn't always that way but it was now. The ache that she'd felt earlier was gone. Like a junkie giving her body a fix, now she could deal with what she had to do. She had to move on in a way that would convince Cash that it was over. She had to do something to convince herself that it was over. She didn't know how she would accomplish this but she knew that she would.

Cash left with his wife and children for Tennessee. A lot of Leah's friends went on this trip. Leah wasn't upset but she hadn't admitted to anyone that she'd given into Cash again. Now more than ever she was convinced that she had to do something drastic to end her relationship with Cash for good. She thought about going back to Detroit for a while but she had to wait until

Christmas break. The thought came to her mind that if she got involved with someone else he would have to leave her alone.

Leah decided to put her plan into affect on Friday. Most of Leah's friends had taken the charter trip to Tennessee that Cash and his wife had gone on so she didn't have anybody to hang out with. She got dressed and walked to the Joint. There were very few people at the club that night. She spoke and danced with a few of the regulars. Just as she was about to declare her self bored and leave Willie Lofton walked into the bar. God he was fine! He was as dark as the black leather jacket he was wearing, with a brilliant white smile that he flashed as soon as he saw Leah.

She smiled back at him giving him the permission he needed to come over to the table where she was sitting with two drinks in his hand. "This is a peace offering" he said with that gorgeous smile he was so famous for. Leah was almost afraid to reach for the drink but she did. "Where is everybody?" he asked looking around at the small crowd. "Tennessee," Leah responded. "Oh yeah, everybody went…," and he stopped in mid sentence when he realized that Cash and his family were on that trip. Leah smiled to let him off the hook.

"What the f#@* is up with the two of you, I'm amazed at the fact that you're sitting here smiling. I'm saying, this bastard is on a trip with his wife and kids and you sitting here waiting on him" Willie was mad all over again. "You said that I didn't" Leah said still smiling. Willie sat there trying to read her. "You're not waiting for him?" he asked. "I'm just hanging out, I'm not waiting for anybody" Leah told him again. Willie motioned for the waiter and ordered another drink. "What are you doing?" he asked looking at her suspiciously. Leah started to laugh and repeated that she was just hanging out.

Willie had a million questions about her and Cash, but his main concern was whether or not they were still together. She assured him that they were not. Willie sat back and took a long look at Leah, "I want to ask you something, but before you answer me I want you to be sure that it is over between you and Cash. There is a party at my complex tonight and I want you to come with me." "A party at your complex?" Leah asked. "Yes, I want you to come with me," Willie took a sip from his drink, "I'll be back in a minute, let me know if you want to come with me."

Leah thought about what would happen if Cash found out that she went with Willie. She didn't come out looking for Willie but he was the perfect solution to her problem. Cash would absolutely die or kill her but it would be over. He would never forgive her, and he would leave her alone. She didn't know why Willie wanted her but it didn't matter, she made up her mind that she would go to the party with Willie and then, whatever.

Willie walked back to the table and asked Leah if she was going. She said yes and they left. Willie did take her to the party. Leah was afraid of what she was about to do so she drank a lot at the party. Willie finally got her to leave but he didn't take her home. They went to his apartment, which was the plan from the beginning. Leah went through the motions, as it turned out Willie was very attentive to her sexual needs. When it was over his phone rang and he went to answer it. He was very different when he came back. "Come on, I'd better take you home," he said. Leah did what he said.

When they got to Leah's house Willie was acting so strange that she asked him what was wrong. He sat there for a minute thinking about what to say, "You know you could very well be one of the smartest, sexiest, mature young women that I know, but you got this weakness for a jackass that I just don't understand. I know that I could make you forget that he ever existed; there is no doubt in my mind. What I can't deal with is you lying to me about it being over for you. You could have told me that you just wanted to have sex with me to get back at him but instead you told me it was over. How can it be over and you was just with him a few nights ago?" He was beyond mad. "Who told you that?" she asked him. "What difference does it make, it's true. Look, I'm not ready to get in the middle of a situation when we both know you gone turn around and go right back to him, get out."

Leah got out of the car hoping that she would be able to explain to him at a later date what had actually happened tonight. She didn't set out to use him but she did set out to find someone to use. She wished it hadn't been him, she didn't really think they could have a serious relationship but she didn't want him as an enemy. One thing was for sure, either Cash knew they had been together or it wouldn't be long before he did. Now all that was left was to wait for the fall out. She would not have to wait long.

Leah spent the rest of the weekend at home. She hung out with her family and waited to hear from Cash. Willie called on Sunday afternoon to warn her that Cash knew they had been together. She used that opportunity to apologize for getting him involved in the first place. When Leah hung up from talking to Willie she was petrified. She did talk to Anna and Gary about what was going on. Gary warned her that he wouldn't take this well but Leah convinced them both that she could handle him. She wanted it over and now it would be.

Gary and Anna left Monday morning warning Leah to be careful. She promised them she would. She got the kids off to school and daycare and waited, the wooden door open and the screen unlocked. At the last minute she strategically placed a hammer and a knife in the unit just in case, she hoped that she wouldn't need it. It wasn't long before Cash showed up. This time he knocked on the door. She saw him from the dining room and told him to come in. She took a seat at the dining room table to make him have to sit across from her, he did. It took him a while before he said anything; he just looked at her.

She had to finally break the silence and ask, "Are you O.K.?" "What difference does it make, what happened between you and Willie?" "You obviously already know what happened," she said defiantly. "No I want to hear you say it, tell me about going out with one of my closest friends." She admitted to him that they went to the party together, he wanted to know what happened after the party. When she started to tell him he stood up from where he was sitting. It happened so fast that Leah didn't have a chance to get to the hammer or knife she had stashed. He came around the table and grabbed her by the neck, backing her up to the wall.

"You are the worst kind of slut, how could you be with me one day and turn around not two days later and be with anybody else, least alone him" he said through clinched teeth. Leah was angry herself now, how dare he call her a slut after the way he'd been acting. His wife, other women, he had a lot of nerve calling her a slut. "I don't know, why don't you ask your wife I'm sure she can explain it to you, that's what she was doing for quite sometime behind your back wasn't she?" Leah wished she could take back the words the minute that she said them.

Cash pushed her head up against the wall and dug his fingers into her neck. "You wanted it over, you got it! Don't ever call me or come near me again" He turned around to leave and walked into the china cabinet, the door popped open and he slammed it back shattering the cabinet door and cutting his arm. "Cash your arm," she said trying to make sure he was O.K. He snatched his arm away "F... you, F... you, don't ever touch me again, if you see me on the street b*#@! act like you don't, because if you even look my way I swear to God I will kill you."

He finally left. Leah looked around at the blood and glass; she cleaned it up thinking about what had just happened. She dreaded calling Anna to tell her about the cabinet but she did. Once she found out that everyone was O.K. she wasn't as upset as Leah thought she would be. She agreed with Leah that that should be the end of the relationship between her and Cash. Now she wanted to know what Leah would do. She thought she should go to Detroit until he calmed down. Somehow, Leah heard, "I'm sick of the drama, go home." She knew she was right but she didn't want to leave. Cash's phone call convinced her she should go. He told her again how much he hated her and how much he wanted to kill her. It was time to go.

Leah spent the next few days hiding in her sister's house and packing her and Bianca's clothes. She didn't want to go home without any money so she stole a set of her sister's old wedding rings and pawned them. Anna and Gary paid for her bus ticket home, took her to the bus station and put her on the bus. All the way back to Detroit she thought about how much things had changed. She wasn't sad or crying, she wasn't scared the way she was when she came to Dayton. It was crazy, the small town had toughened her up in a way the big city could not have.

She was going back to the city a woman. She would never fall in love again, never be vulnerable to another man. If they couldn't take care of her and her daughter, she didn't have anything for them. Unless of course she had some physical needs, then she would look for someone who could fill them and go home. She was done with love. As the bus left the station she told herself that she would be O.K., she had a plan. She would never be anyone's victim again. There were no more tears to shed, she held onto Bianca and went to sleep. She would literally wake up in the next chapter of her life and she was looking forward to it.

CHAPTER TWENTY-EIGHT

The first few months of being home were uneventful for Leah. She wasn't sure where she was going or what she wanted to do. She knew that she didn't want to think about the life that she'd left behind. She knew that it was the right thing to break up with Cash but she hated the way she'd done it. When she allowed herself to think about it, it hurt a lot. She missed him so much the ache was almost physical so she began to relieve the pain the only way she knew how. It was nothing serious at first, or so she told herself. It wouldn't be long though before she was drinking and drugging every night.

Leah had come home and moved back in with Momma. Things were a lot different than when she left, Momma had made lots of new friends and was partying every night herself. It wasn't long before Leah found a live in position with a young woman who turned out to be a local dancer. Once she'd taken the job Leah became more involved in the nightly party scene. She became more of a friend to the young woman than an employee and they began to hang out together. A few months later the young woman became ill and had to move back in with her Mom but not before Leah was introduced to all of the players at a night spot called The Pink Poodle. This became Leah's new hangout.

Leah moved back in with her sister Jean and continued to party almost every night. She met new people who introduced her to more players and she became quite comfortable playing the street life game. She was pretty good at the game too. She met an ex-convict named Tony who was very sweet to her in the beginning but who later became very possessive and violent. He did whatever he wanted to do, went wherever he wanted to go, but didn't want Leah to go anywhere or do anything. She quickly grew tired of this so on a Saturday night she defied him and went out with her friends.

She didn't think that he would look for her until after the clubs were closed but unfortunately she was wrong. Everywhere he looked for her she had already been there and was gone so by Sunday morning Tony was very angry. Leah hadn't known him very long so she didn't know what he was capable of. He showed up acting as if he were not very angry and offered to take her to breakfast. Once alone he started to grill her about where she was and with who the night before. She told him the truth but he thought that she was lying and they argued.

Tony stopped at a gas station to get drinks for them and continued driving in a direction Leah didn't recognize. Immediately her radar was alerted. Tony pulled into a construction site but it was Sunday morning and no one was there. He drove to the furthest end of the site and stopped the car. Again he began to accuse Leah of being with someone else and again she denied it. Before she knew it he had his hands around her neck and was squeezing. It only took a few seconds for her to realize that he was seriously trying to kill her and her reaction was just as quick. She picked up the bottle of Coke that he'd bought her to drink and with everything in her, smashed him on the head with it.

Blood spewed everywhere, she'd felt some pain in her hand as the bottle broke, she didn't know if the blood was coming from her hand or his head and she didn't care. She opened the door, jumped from the car and started running. She never looked back until she saw the police car. She began to flag them down but to her surprise they'd come looking for a couple that was reported to be on that construction site without permission. She quickly told the officers what was happening.

Tony was still sitting in his car trying to stop his head from bleeding when the officers went back, arrested him, and sent him back to prison for a parole violation. Some months later she would spot him at a red light. She was terrified at first but fear was soon replaced with defiance. He looked at her as if he was looking through her but somewhere she found the courage t o meet his gaze. She could see that he'd had to have stitches in his head and that made her even more defiant. She'd heard that he was out and asking around for her but by then she was friends with a couple of guys from a local motorcycle club called 'The Sons of the Zodiac' who had warned him to stay away from her. Tony's stare turned into a smile and like the coward that he was, he pulled off and she never saw him again.

The next few months were so much fun or so Leah thought. Jean had made friends with a young lady named Carmen who had a younger sister,

Carol. The four of them had become the closest of friends and spent the next months hanging out together. Jean was married by now but she and her husband fought a lot about how much she hung out and the fact that she wasn't taking care of him and his house. Jean didn't care she just wanted to hang out.

Jean and Carol had taken a job at a neighborhood restaurant called Sonny's. Sonny was a neighborhood character that owned a record shop and restaurant right next door to each other. He was also one of the biggest dope men in Detroit at the time. He was also a married man with two young sons that worked closely with him. Leah would go to the restaurant to sit and wait for Jean and Carol to get off work so they could hang out. Sonny decided the first time he'd seen Leah that she would belong to him but he had to take his time because his wife also spent a great deal of time at the restaurant.

They would fight all the time about all of the women that hung around. She'd left the restaurant one night stating out loud that she was tired of all these women hanging around that weren't buying anything. She'd made the statement on her way out of the door directing her comment to Leah who just stared at her defiantly. Sonny had come from his office just in time to witness the exchange. Leah never said a word she didn't have to. Her body language spoke pure defiance as she glared back at Sonny's wife.

This was a game that Leah had become a master at. The looks and comments from Sonny's wife made her more determined that she would be with this woman's husband. She'd become quite comfortable being the other woman. The mind games had become second nature to her but now she'd become ready and willing to take it into the physical realm. She was not afraid of this woman and everything within her conveyed that message.

The woman stopped to talk to her son, still eyeing Leah. Leah continued to meet the woman's gaze until she looked away, probably figuring that Leah was one of Sonny's crazy motorcycle gang friends. Leah turned around after the woman left to find Sonny looking quite pleased with himself. The defiant look turned toward him; little did he know that she had no plans of becoming the other woman just because he was the infamous Sonny White. The raised eyebrow and the tilted head should have warned him that he'd be in for a rude awakening.

Leah had no intention of ever falling in love with another man. But Cash had been nothing else but thorough in teaching her how to get and keep a man's attention. If this was the hand she'd been dealt, she'd play it to the max. Oh yeah, she would be the other woman, but it would cost them. Everything she did for any man from this day forward would be strictly to her advantage. If they weren't willing to pay the price, in the infamous words of a toast her mother often made to her friends, "Two brothers living upon the hill, if one wont, the other one will, here's to his brother," which she would follow with one word, "NEXT." It would not be long before Sonny White would begin to understand the kind of woman he'd decided he wanted.

CHAPTER TWENTY-NINE

The one thing Leah had become accustomed to was the party life. Sonny understood that, he began to take her with him to the motorcycle gang to show her off. He also became her main source for the marijuana that she'd begun to smoke more frequently. He not only supplied her but made sure that she had enough to supply her friends as well. She was beginning to take advantage of him in every way that she could. She would take his drugs and his money but she would not sleep with him. It would not take long for him to get tired of the situation, but when he did she would not skip a beat.

Leah and her friends had begun to hang out at a local club called the "Pink Poodle." They went out every weekend for a couple of months straight getting high almost every day. Leah was starting to grow tired of the party life for several reasons, first and foremost was that she was not spending a lot of time with Bianca. She'd really started to miss her baby girl who was spending a lot of time with Momma.

One Saturday morning Leah woke up having stayed out all night with Carol who had become her closest friend. She looked around the flat where Carol stayed to see beer and liquor bottles strewn everywhere, not to mention the cocktails from all the marijuana they'd smoked the night before. She glanced down at her fingertips that were black from a combination of marijuana and opium she'd been smoking. Her head hurt, probably from lack of sleep and too much drugs and alcohol and Bianca was nowhere around. She missed her baby terribly and decided that she would go to Momma's today to spend some time with her daughter.

Leah tried to get a ride but everyone told her to wait until later. She tried to lie down and go back to sleep but every time she closed her eyes she saw her baby girl so she got up, showered and got dressed. She was so determined to get to her daughter that she decided she would catch the bus. She took great effort to fix her self up so she wouldn't look so run down when she saw her baby girl. Leah stepped outside and saw the clouds but that didn't stop her, she was determined to see her baby.

She walked the short distance to the bus stop and stood there waiting for the bus. She'd not been standing there ten minutes when the drizzle started. Her mind told her she could make it back to Carol's before she was completely soaked but she knew that if she did another round of getting high would start and she would not get to see her baby today so she looked around for shelter. As she was looking around for shelter she saw the blue Catalina slow down, look at her and keep going. She realized she was not far from the store where they bought their liquor so she headed there to stand in the doorway and wait for the bus.

She just made it to the store before it started to pour down raining. A few minutes later the blue Catalina was back but instead of slowing down they stopped at the store and got out. The man appeared to be a gentle giant of sorts far different from the rough neck men that Leah had become accustomed to meeting since she'd started hanging out. He smiled at her as he passed her to go into the store and she smiled back. She'd just settled in her mind that she wasn't the type of woman this man was looking for when he came back out of the store spoke to her and asked if she needed a ride.

Leah told herself that she was accepting the ride to get out of the rain and to hurry and get to her baby but something about this man made her curious. He was friendly and kind and she didn't have to be hard-core with him. He was genuinely concerned about her being stranded in the rain. He was so different than the men she'd been dealing with and it was refreshing. He introduced himself, asked where she was going and she told him. Leah immediately felt safe with him. Not only did she feel he wouldn't hurt her but she felt like he would keep her safe from any other harm.

They made small talk as he drove her to Momma's house to see Bianca. Once there they sat outside and talked for a while before she invited him in to meet her family. It was as if she'd known him forever. Her family liked him immediately; he laughed and joked with them as if he were already a part of the family. Leah was in heaven; she was with her baby girl and actually laughing and having fun with her family. Chuck stayed with her for a while, asked for her number and left. If she never saw him again she would always be grateful for the past couple of hours.

It would not be long before she would hear from him again. Later on that day she got a call from him inviting her to go bowling with him. Wow, an actual date, something she couldn't ever remember doing. Leah gladly accepted the invitation and began to prepare for the date. Chuck showed up when he said he would however when they got to the bowling alley it was league night so Chuck suggested they go back to his place and hang out with his friends. Leah was reluctant but she accepted the invitation.

When they got to his place Leah was pleasantly surprised. It was a beautiful flat right in the same neighborhood where Leah had grown so accustomed to the party life. Once there, true to his word Chuck called over some of his friends to play cards and hang out. Desire and Jimmy from the upstairs flat, Veronica and Daniel, sisters from across the street all came to check out Chuck's new friend. They were having a good time listening to music, laughing and dancing when Chuck declared that Leah was no longer a visitor and had to wait on herself from now on like everybody else.

Leah went to the refrigerator opened it and began to laugh. There was nothing in the refrigerator but bologna, peanut butter, and tons of beer. When she'd met Chuck earlier he had driven by the store slowly and come back around the corner, parked and went into the store. Leah had decided in her mind that he must have been looking for a parking space when he slowed down. Chuck had went into the store, bought one beer and come back out to ask her if she needed a ride, but now she was looking in his refrigerator and seeing more beer than she'd ever seen in one persons refrigerator letting her know that his stop at the store was a ploy all the long.

She got herself a beer and walked back into the dining room. She must have had a strange look on her face because Chuck noticed and asked what was wrong. "Nothing," she lied, with a big stupid grin on her face, but he pressed her for an answer. She finally answered him by saying "There is a lot of beer in that refrigerator." Chuck looked puzzled for a moment, and then they both began to laugh. "It worked didn't it?" and they both continued to laugh. By now every one else realized that whatever was going on was an inside joke but they still laughed.

It was getting late and company started leaving, Leah was as close to what she thought was heaven than she'd ever been in her life. Everybody was gone except her and Chuck and they were sharing the remnants of the evening laughing about Chuck's friends and making small talk. They sat together on the sofa, which was a beautiful plush sectional, had another beer and talked about what happened that night. When they seemed to run out of words to say Chuck got serious, "I know that I should take you home now, but I don't want to."

Leah met his gaze but only for a moment, she took a deep breath. It would be nothing for her to stay, she'd grown used to doing whatever she wanted but she knew this was a different kind of man and she didn't want to scare him away by having sex with him on the very first night. She laid her head on his chest for a moment. When she looked up at him she'd fought off the urge to give in to what he wanted, what they both wanted. She told him that even though she wanted to stay with him that night she had to leave. He gave her one final hug, the only way to describe it would be kin to a bear hug, kissed her and stood up pulling her up with him, "Then we'd better hit the road."

Chuck drove her back to her mother's house with a cyclone of feelings going on inside her mind. Chuck was definitely one of the good guys, ready and willing to do anything he had to do to have Leah in his life. Leah enjoyed being with him but there was something missing. She didn't want to use him as she did the other guys who so obviously wanted only one thing but the passion that she'd experienced before was not there for him.

Chuck was nine years older than Leah and worked for Chrysler. He made a good living at his job and could well afford to take care of Leah and Bianca and he wanted to do just that. He was from a good family; his parents had been married for over twenty-five years. He had two sisters that loved him dearly. They were so different than the family that Leah had come from. Chuck wanted the same kind of family that his parents had.

Although Leah enjoyed being with Chuck when they were together, she still longed for the party life. In fact even though she and Chuck had become an item she was still hanging out with her friends. Things had begun to happen between them so fast that Leah had forgotten to ask the important questions. Chuck lived alone so why would she in a million years believe that he was a married man.

Chuck had chosen to keep this bit of information from Leah. He had gotten married less than a year ago but the woman that he'd married decided she didn't want to be his wife after all. That is until she heard that he was with someone else. Leah would find out the hard way that even the nicest guys could be the biggest liars. She and Chuck were lying around watching T.V.

when the doorbell rang. Chuck went to the door and Leah continued laying there watching the movie. She didn't even think twice when he didn't come right back from the door.

About twenty minutes had past before Leah realized that Chuck had not come back from the door so she got up to see what was going on. She got to the dining room just in time to hear him tell his wife that this was not her home and that she had to leave. He was with someone else now and this was her house. Leah walked into the living room where they were talking, Chuck took that opportunity to introduce his woman to his wife. The first she'd ever heard that the woman existed.

Leah was shocked at what she'd heard but she had experienced enough drama in her young life not to tip her hand. She smiled at the woman who didn't seem to be as clueless as she was pretending to be. Leah flipped her bi*#@ switch and pretended to be happy to meet her. The woman turned to Chuck and asked for a ride someplace. Chuck looked at Leah as if to ask for permission. Of course she would let him take her away from there, but there would be hell to pay when he got back. Leah stood there as they prepared to leave. The woman had brought all of her clothes with her thinking that she was coming to move in. Leah stood defiantly as they picked up all of her things and went out of the door, got into the car and left.

Once they were gone Leah decided that all would be fair from this day forward. He was a liar just like all of the rest of them and he would pay for his deception. She had really come to trust Chuck and enjoyed the mock family life they shared together. As far as Leah was concerned this was carde blanche to do whatever she wanted and stay with Chuck. He never should have betrayed her this way. Just when she thought that she could trust someone he would have to pull this. She poured herself a drink and went back into the room to wait. She decided that she would teach him a lesson so she got dressed and called Sonny White to come pick her up.

When she finally did come home he was so happy to see her that he didn't even question her about where she'd been. He apologized to her for not telling her about his wife and swore that he only wanted to be with her and had asked his wife for a divorce. That would have been fine except he came home the very next weekend smelling as if he'd had sex with someone else. At this point Leah didn't even care; she had a beautiful home, a nice car, money and permission to hang out whenever she wanted.

As it turned out since Chuck and his first wife never actually lived together so they were able to get a quick annulment. He would have done anything to keep Leah happy at the time. He wanted to be wherever she was and wanted her with him all the time. It had gotten to the point he didn't want her out of his sight for very long. At this point he had to settle knowing that whenever she got tired of partying she would come home to him.

Leah continued to see Sonny and J.D., both members of the same motorcycle club and both married with plenty of money. The betrayal that she'd suffered finding out that Chuck was married put him in the same category as the rest of the men who'd lied to her. Oh, she would stay but it would be on her own terms. She would do what she wanted, when she felt like it. One thing that she could count on was that he would do anything to keep her happy at this point and she would take advantage of that for as long as she could. Little did she know that she would end up loving him enough to want to have a family with him.

CHAPTER THIRTY

Chrysler announced they would close the plant where Chuck worked which was fine with him since by now he hardly ever went to work anymore. He spent most of his time spoiling Leah and the rest of the time waiting for her to come home. With money tight they moved out of their flat and into the basement of a house owned by one of Leah's party crew. By then one night had begun to run into the other and Chuck was following behind Leah like a lost puppy.

Gary and Anna really liked Chuck so on one of their visits home Gary talked Chuck into joining the armed forces. Chuck was a big guy so the army accepted him with the stipulation that he would drop some weight before he would actually be allowed to enter boot camp. Gary convinced Chuck that he would stand a better chance of losing the weight if he came to Ohio and allowed him to mentor him through the process.

It was a good idea for everyone; Anna and Gary actually missed having Leah around. They were surprised to find out that things ran a lot more smoothly when Leah was there. Having her there had given them freedoms that they'd taken for granted until she was gone. Now she and Chuck were moving in with them. Leah was excited to move back, as good as Chuck had been to her she still missed Cash and looked forward to the opportunity to see him again.

He and his wife were back together in every way but neither he nor Leah cared at this point. Now they were on an even playing field as they were both with other people now and had something to lose if they did not behave. In a sense, things had gotten back to normal in Page Manor. Cash, Ernie and their wives were at the very least pleasant with Anna and Gary and Ann had warned Leah that she wanted to keep it that way. At this point Leah thought she wanted what they had. She thought that she too would marry a soldier and be able to do whatever she wanted as she'd seen done with each of the military families that she'd been acquainted with.

It would not take long before Leah and Cash would see each other again, it was inevitable. Leah just had no idea to what extreme Cash would go to, or how bold he would become when it came to her. In Cash's mind Leah still belonged to him and no one could change that. He'd convinced himself that no man could take his place in Leah's life and he was right. Leah would never love nor give herself so completely and naively to any man, especially not the one that broken her heart into so many pieces.

Chuck was preparing to go out for a jog when the doorbell rang. Leah was upstairs putting the girls down for a nap when so Chuck went to the door. Leah could not believe the next sound that she heard. "Is Leah here?," she heard Cash ask. Chuck wasn't sure who the two guys were that was asking for Leah, but he didn't feel threatened at all. He and Leah were there for each other now. He had all the faith that Leah would be with him no matter what. They had gone through a rough year with him losing his job and their place to live and she had been behind every decision to help him pick up the pieces of his life. He wasn't worried about who they were. "Yeah, she's here, Leah somebody is here for you," Chuck said right before he went out of the door for his jog.

By the time Leah got down the stairs Cash and Uncle Ernie were sitting at the dining room table opening the lunch they'd brought with them. Uncle Ernie was the first one to speak to Leah. He stood up and acknowledged how drop dead gorgeous she'd become over the last year. He was openly teasing Cash now by telling her as much. "Damn girl, you look good, your man must be doing all of the right things to and for you," he said laughing at Cash.

Cash barely looked up, he didn't want to stare and he didn't have to. He could see at a glance that what Ernie was saying was true. Leah was svelte, buxom, and drop dead gorgeous. He kept rattling around with his lunch as if he were looking for something. "Hello," Leah said forcing him to look at her. Cash looked up from what he was doing momentarily, "Hey, could you get me some salt?" he finally said staring at her defiantly as if he'd just saw her that morning. They all started to laugh, "Sure, but when I show up at your door asking for things from your wife's kitchen I want you to be just as cordial."

"Oh, is this his kitchen? I thought that I was at my friends house" he said referring to Gary and Anna. "You are so funny," Leah said as she went into the kitchen to get the salt. She came back into the dining room with the salt and sat down at the table. There was an awkward silence at the table before Ernie began to talk again. He told Leah that Michelle had gone back to Florida because her Mom was sick and brought her up to speed on all of their friends. They kept the conversation going for a few minutes before they seemed to run out of things to say. Cash purposely did not talk in an effort to make the reunion difficult.

It was hard for him as they were sitting at the same dining room table, as they had been when he found out that Leah had sex with his friend. She and Ernie had talked about everyone except Willie Lofton. Cash was happy to see her, if he had his way he would take her down into Dayton and make love to her well into the night but he knew that would open Pandora's Box and he was afraid of what would happen. He was back with his wife and Leah was with this new guy. He hated the thought of Leah being with another man.

He kept quiet because he was afraid of what he might say. His emotions were all over the place; he still loved her, and missed her tremendously. He wanted to tell her that but she was with someone else now, someone that seemed to be making her happy. This man seemed very confident in his relationship with Leah and Cash just wasn't sure if she still felt the same way about him as he obviously still felt about her. All of the pain had come flooding back into his heart. For the first time since they'd gotten there the seriousness of the situation came to the surface. It was time for them to leave and go back to work so Ernie hugged her and said goodbye.

Once he left, the awkwardness returned. Cash looked at her and for the first time Leah saw hurt instead of anger. She wanted to fall into his arms and pretend that the past year had never happened but she had made a vow never to love him or any other man that way again. Cash was the first to break the silence, "It really is good to see you." Leah had not been this afraid in a very long time. "It's good to see you too." Cash held out his hand to her and she took it. He pulled her to him and held her there. They both took deep breaths and held each other for a moment. Leah tried to pull away but Cash would not let go.

"I just need to know for sure that you are alright," Cash told her. Leah assured him that she was O.K. They talked for a few minutes about how each other were and promised to talk again soon. Leah was so relieved when he left, she sat down at the table and all the memories came flooding back to her. How much they'd fought, how mean they were to each other, and how in the end he'd gone back to his wife. The hurt was fresh all over again.

Leah was deep in thought when Chuck came back. She was genuinely happy to see him. She was safe with him. She didn't worry about him choosing someone else, he'd chosen her; and she could trust that. Chuck walked in looking for a cue to say something dumb, but he saw the serious look on her face and walked toward her. Leah didn't want him to know what she was feeling at the time so she shook herself and pretended to be O.K. He asked anyway and she lied. No one would get to her that way ever again, at least they wouldn't know if they did.

CHAPTER THIRTY-ONE

Chuck went to work for a local gas station as an attendant. He and Leah moved out of Anna and Gary's house and got their own place. Leah had grown to love and depend on him very much, and against everything that she'd promised herself, she'd begun to trust him. He continued to work on his weight to meet the Army's requirements but he was very secretive. One thing was for certain, Chuck loved Leah and he would do anything to prove it to her including deceiving her.

He learned very early in their relationship that if he could not give her what she wanted, she would simply get it from someplace else, mainly, Cash Windsor. Cash was still very much in love with Leah and would do anything for her. He took great pleasure in giving her things that he knew Chuck could not afford. Leah would soon learn that Chuck always wanted to look good in her eyes and would do just about anything to stay in her good graces.

They'd made a pretty decent life for themselves up until the now. Cash found out that he was to receive an award at an annual dinner dance given by the local VFW. He wanted Leah to be there even though he would be there with his wife. Carla didn't care, for all intensive purposes Leah had been instrumental in giving her family back and that was all that she cared about. Cash gave Leah two tickets to the banquet and told her to bring Chuck. Leah had a lot of friends on program and wanted to attend but didn't have anything to wear; of course Cash took care of that which really upset Chuck.

When they got to the dance Leah was reacquainted with a lot of her old friends that she had not seen since she had returned to Dayton. Although she introduced Chuck to them he still felt out of place, these were friends of Leah and Cash's and they were all amazed that the two of them were in the same room with other people and were not trying to kill each other. It was a lot of fun for Leah and Cash but Chuck and Carla were not having very much fun at all. Leah was genuinely trying to include Chuck in the evening but Cash was doing all that he could to let both he and Carla know that Leah was still his and there was nothing that either of them could do about it.

Chuck and Cash had seen each other in passing, knew whom each other were but had not been formerly introduced. Chuck decided to play a few mind games of his own, he went over to the table where Cash and his party were sitting, extended his hand and introduced himself. Cash had watched him cross the room and even though he wanted to hit him he stood up accepted Chuck's hand, smiled and introduced himself and everybody at the table. Leah watched the exchange shaking her head in unbelief. She knew that Chuck could be devious but she had not expected him to try to rub in Cash's face the fact that they were there together.

It took a while before Leah realized what Cash was doing and when she did she thought it was cute. As if the looks he'd been giving her all night were not enough he manipulated the situation so that he could speak to her alone to tell her exactly what he was feeling. Some of the Air Force wives were performing a belly dance routine; one of those wives was a good friend of Leah's. Snow was the kind of woman who did what she wanted whenever she wanted. In fact up until tonight, Cash had never wanted Leah to hang out with Snow but he needed her tonight and he had a way of convincing people to do what he wanted.

He asked Snow to get Leah backstage to help with the costumes and hair; they really did need the help so Snow asked her. Leah was thrilled to be asked to help which meant that Chuck would be left sitting without a date. Cash took great pride in coming to the table to tell Leah that she was needed in the back to help the ladies, and also to apologize to Chuck for taking away his date. It was O.K. Chuck reminded him, "I get to take her home," he and Leah laughed but Cash did not think the comment very funny, although he let it slide without saying anything.

He knew that Leah had feelings for this man, perhaps even loved him but it wasn't arrogance that told him their relationship lacked the passion he shared with Leah. Even now he and Leah both knew that if he pushed the issue she would leave with him tonight and Chuck's comment may very well have caused him to make that decision. Leah was beautiful tonight in the dress that he'd bought her; they were there with tickets that he'd provided. Cash was starting to convince himself that Chuck could not take care of

Leah, not in the way she deserved, not in any way. He smiled a devious smile and simply said "Yeah." Leah watched him walk back to his table and sit down, the look on his face told her that he was about to do something that they both may end up regretting.

Leah went in the back to help the ladies, she and Snow were back there cutting up, laughing about Leah's situation. "I don't know what you got under that skirt, but you need to bottle and sell it," they both laughed. Snow was talking to her when Cash approached, Leah noticed Snow looking over her shoulder and turned to see what she was looking at. Cash approached the two of them and spoke to Snow as if for the first time, Snow spoke and made an excuse to leave the two of them alone.

"Hey," Leah said to him. "Hey yourself, you O.K.?" Cash asked her. "Yeah, why do you ask?" Leah was curious about his demeanor. Cash looked at her as if he were trying to look through her, "I don't like your friend," he finally said. "I'm sure that the feeling is mutual but why do you say that?" Leah asked him. Cash answered her question with one of his own, "Is he taking care of you?" "What do you mean?" Leah was confused. "It's a simple enough question, is he taking care of you?" Leah just stood there looking at him. Cash touched her neck in that spot that he knew would drive her crazy, "Does he know about this?" he asked never once smiling, Leah moved his hand away, "Please don't do that," she told him defiantly. "Well that answers one part of my question, do you and Bianca have everything that you need?" "That's not your concern anymore Cash," Leah tried to convince him that she didn't want anything from him anymore but she wasn't convinced so it wasn't working.

Cash stood there for a moment weighing what he was about to say. "You and Bianca will always be my concern," his closeness was starting to get uncomfortable

So Leah pushed pass him and went back to helping the ladies. Cash returned to the party with a new confidence that did nor get past Chuck. In fact when he passed the table where Chuck sat he couldn't help but to stop and talk to his friends, none of which Chuck knew very well. The look in Chuck's eyes wasn't as confident as it was when he'd visited Cash's table earlier. Cash did not pass up the opportunity to exchange looks and ask if Chuck were enjoying himself on his way back to his own table.

When Cash got back to his own table he found his wife drinking and acting as if everything was O.K. Why shouldn't she feel that way, she knew her husband was very much in love with Leah, but she also knew that Leah had done everything she could to get Cash to leave her and none of it had worked. She knew that in his own way, Cash loved her and he adored his children and nothing she could do or say would change that. Cash just was not the kind of man that would walk away from his family that she was confident of. If he were going to leave her he'd have left by now. They could flirt all they wanted, they could even get together if they wanted eventually Cash was coming home.

Leah made her way back to the table a few minutes later. Chuck was not very happy about the looks that were exchanged between she and Cash. Nor was he happy about how she'd left him sitting alone at the table for so long. Leah had never experienced his anger directed toward her so she didn't know how to handle it. He was very quiet which was definitely out of character for him. Leah sat next to him and held his hand, "Don't let him get to you," she told him calmly. "Well it's too late for that," he told her not trying to hide his anger. "Listen," Leah said to him "Let me tell you something, that is over, he made his choice and I made mine."

Chuck looked at her and smiled, he knew that she meant what she was saying. He also knew that there was still something between the two of them. But for tonight, she would belong to him and that gave him comfort. He hugged her close. Leah looked over her shoulder too and caught the look of disapproval from across the room. Cash made no attempt to hide his contempt from anyone, including his wife who remained oblivious to what was going on. Cash picked up his drink and feigned a toast towards Leah, the look in his eyes brought back chilly memories, but she shot him back a look of her own that told him to back off.

CHAPTER THIRTY-TWO

Leah and Chuck made it through the party. Chuck continued to work on his weight and was making progress. His job at the gas station was enough to pay the bills they were accumulating but they'd left a lot back in Detroit, which was about to catch up with them. What Leah didn't realize until it was almost too late is that Chuck would do anything not to upset her including not tell her that he'd lost his job and that they were threatening to repossess their car. That information would come in the middle of a cold night when Leah least expected it.

A week or so before they would actually take back the car Leah and Chuck were ready to leave for the morning. Chuck would drop Leah off at beauty college, and he and Bianca would hang out together until it was time for Leah to get out of school. They would pick Leah up from school and then Chuck would go to the gas station where he worked the afternoon shift. On this particular morning they were having trouble getting the car started. Chuck thought it wouldn't start because of how cold it was and he was partially right.

He continued to try to start the car until they both heard a noise that sounded as if something literally cracked under the hood. They didn't know what had happened, Leah went into the house and called Sarah for a ride to school. By the time she came home from school that night she would learn that the engine block on the car was cracked. The mechanic told Chuck it was because the temperature had dropped suddenly and there was only water in the radiator, it would costs hundreds of dollars to fix. Leah didn't know how they would get it fixed but Chuck had already come up with a plan in his mind to get the money.

A few nights later, Leah got up to get a drink from the kitchen and heard some noise outside of the kitchen door. She peeked outside the kitchen window and saw headlight coming from a truck. She followed the headlight to their car where there was a man under the hood of their car. By the time she woke up Chuck and they got to the back yard the man was hitching the car to a tow truck. Chuck went to talk to the man, who gave him some official papers of repossession. Evidently the mechanic had found out there was a lien on the car and had given the finance company their address.

Chuck didn't know what to do, he had to tell her the truth now, and when he did Leah flipped out. "Why didn't you tell me, we could have gone without something else!!!" Chuck tried to explain that he didn't tell her because he didn't want to upset her but she continued to scream at him saying. "And you didn't think them taking the car would upset me, that is just stupid!!!" Leah could not calm down, she felt as if she'd been betrayed, Chuck felt as if he was trying to protect her from worrying. He tried to comfort her but she would not let him come any where near her, his worse fears had come true, she didn't want anything to do with him.

He was so sure that she was going to go call Cash and tell him everything but she didn't. She'd told Cash that Chuck was more than capable of taking care of them and she wanted nothing more to do with him. He was back with his wife, she was with Chuck and that was that. Leah didn't want anyone to know that they were struggling so she only told the part about the engine block being cracked to her family and friends. She was determined that Cash or anyone else would not get to tell her that she'd made the wrong choice.

She continued going to school getting rides from friends and even catching the bus if she had to. Chuck continued leaving the house everyday as if he were going to work but Leah would soon find out that was a lie as well. Evidently when the car broke down Chuck had come up with the master plan of taking the money they needed to fix the car from his job. Of course they'd found out and fired him. Since they'd taken the car, Chuck had used the money to buy things for Leah and Bianca in an effort to win her back to him.

Now the money and the job were gone and he was forced to pretend to be going to work when he no longer had a job. Instead of telling Leah the truth, which meant another disappointment, he kept up the pretense. Had he told her the truth, she could have gotten someone to keep Bianca during the day so that he could look for another job, but he didn't. He just didn't want to look bad in her eyes. He was able to keep up the lie for a while because he'd stolen the money from work, now he had to come up with a new plan and he did.

Chuck had worked for Chrysler for a long time and had accumulated a lot of luxuries. Leah had not paid attention to the fact that things were beginning to come up missing from their flat. Chuck had begun to pawn or sell everything that was of any value for their every day needs. The bills were no longer being paid, including the rent but Chuck couldn't bring himself to tell her. It would all come to a head soon enough and she would have to go back to her family and friends just to have a place for her and Bianca to stay.

Leah was feeling sick at school one day and decided to leave early which meant she had to catch the bus home. At her transfer point she got off the bus just in time to see her connection driving away from the stop. This meant she had a thirty-minute wait for the next bus. Leah found a bench and sat down. Her mind was wondering all over the place, she'd begun to think about Cash a lot lately. How much easier things had been when she was with him. She never had to worry about a ride or money or even a sitter for Bianca, He always came through for her in those areas.

She was starting to remind herself about the heartache that she'd suffered at the hands of Cash. She'd just convinced herself that this was a better kind of hard because at least Chuck belonged to her and she didn't have to share him with another women, when she saw her connecting bus come up the other side of the street. This snapped her back into the present and she began to gather herself. She knew the bus only had to go a couple of blocks and turn around to get her. She watched as the bus stopped on the other side of the street and Chuck get off.

He wasn't quite alone as he had their two ceramic giraffes in his hand as he walked into the pawnshop across the street. Leah was confused, what was he doing with the giraffes, and where was her baby? She walked across the street and got into the pawnshop just in time to see the owner give Chuck cash for the giraffes. His back was to her, she couldn't believe it, as she looked around the pawnshop she began to recognize her things, the stereo, (which he claimed was in the shop, what a joke), their camera and some other art was decorating the walls of the pawn shop. She just stood there confused. "Can I help you?" the man behind the desk asked her and Chuck turned around to see who he was talking to. Leah ran out of the store just in time to hop on the bus, Chuck of course missed the bus.

Leah got to a seat and sat there, terrified. Who was this person she'd decided to trust? She wanted to rub in everybody's face that she'd finally found someone who only wanted her but what kind of monster was he? She didn't know what but she knew something was very wrong. "Where is my baby?" she heard herself say out loud. Now she was really in a panic. When the bus got to her stop, she jumped off and ran to the flat. She paid no attention to the quiet, she ran straight for the bedroom looking for her baby. Leah saw Bianca laying in her bed and walked over to her. She was sleeping like the angel that she was. Leah pulled back the covers and picked up her baby. She sat down on the bed and began to cry. What had she gotten herself into?

She'd been so afraid for Bianca during the ride home, but how could she believe that Chuck would do anything to hurt their baby. She knew he loved them but she was so confused. Lately it had been one lie after another and she couldn't take much more. Bianca woke up and looked at her mother crying. Leah snuggled her close, "Whats-a-matter Mommy?" Bianca asked in a sleepy voice. Leah tried to assure her that everything was OK but at this point Bianca was doing most of the assuring. "Daddy said not to worry, he said the lights were going to come back on by the time I wake up, he said I had to be a big girl and go to sleep until he fixed the lights, are the lights fixed Mommy?"

Leah couldn't believe what she was hearing, she walked over to the TV and tried to turn it on but there was no electricity. She didn't want Bianca to worry or think bad about Chuck. One thing was for sure, he loved Bianca and she loved him. "No sweetie, they are not back on yet, and they might not come back on tonight. What do you think about us going to stay with Auntie Anna and Na-Na tonight?" Leah asked her knowing how much she loved her Auntie and cousin and knowing that was something that would make her happy without making her worry.

Just as she thought, Bianca was excited about going to Anna's and they went about the flat getting ready making a game out of preparing. Leah called Anna and told her the lights were out, she didn't give her all of the details but that was enough for Anna who was not about to have her niece "over there in that mess." She told Leah to come and to bring the baby. It went without saying that as long as Chuck was not taking care of his responsibilities, he was not welcome.

Anna and Gary had long since begun to see things in Chuck that Leah either couldn't or wouldn't see and Gary had forbid Anna to say anything, to let them work it out on their own. They had no idea of the depths of deception Chuck had gone to, he even owed them money and had sworn them to secrecy. Gary knew that Chuck was out of work only because he'd gone to the gas station on several occasions when Chuck was supposed to be working. When he wasn't there Gary had inquired and been told that he no longer worked there. When Gary found out that Leah and the baby were coming back he wondered what had taken them this long.

Leah and Bianca were pretending they were packing for "an airplane trip" as Bianca called it when Chuck finally came into the house. He wanted to tell her everything before her sister and brother-in-law told her but she didn't want to hear anything he had to say at this point. She could probably forgive him the lies but he'd left her baby in the house alone and for that she would never forgive him. "This is the very reason that I didn't want to tell you," he said to her. "I knew that you would be upset, I knew you wouldn't understand, please baby don't go, the lights will be back on tomorrow just stay so we can talk." Chuck begged her but she was beyond hearing anything he had to say.

Leah didn't know the half of what was going on. When Gary pulled up she grabbed her baby's hand and one of the bags and started toward the door. Chuck came behind her and picked up the other bag. He knew enough about her to know that she'd made up her mind and there was nothing he could do to stop her from leaving. He walked her to the van and put the bags in, then he picked up Bianca and gave her a bug hug. Leah's heart was breaking but she had to go. She didn't know what to expect from him anymore and she wasn't about to stay in the dark with a man she no longer trusted. Chuck put Bianca in her arms and asked Leah to call him when she felt like talking. Leah got in the van and Gary pulled off. Leah noticed that Gary didn't have anything to say to Chuck, he seemed to be as upset with him as she was and Leah would soon find out why.

When Leah got to her sisters house it brought back a flood of memories. The heartbreaks, the attempted rape as well as all of the good times she'd had in that unit. She wasn't sure what was going to happen but she felt safe, maybe for the first time in a long time. She put the girls to bed, laughed and joked with her older nieces and nephew before they went up and finally ended up alone in the den. Anna and Gary came down to talk to her. Gary had decided that it was time Leah knew what they knew. Anna told her about

Photo by: Motown Portrait

HENRY FORD ACADEMY: SCHOOL FOR CREATIVE STUDIES
COMMENCEMENT - JUNE 11, 2013
DETROIT OPERA HOUSE

Rashid Faisal, Principal

Job#: 281424-5 COPYRIGHT 2013
Job#: 408: 0171G5:10:0:0

the borrowed money and the fact that Chuck didn't have a job anymore. How he'd almost gone to jail for stealing the money from his job and that evidently this was not the first time he'd left Bianca home alone.

Leah knew her sister and brother-in-law would not lie to her but she did not want to believe what they were telling her. When she began to think back and to put the pieces together, she knew they were telling the truth. But where did this leave her? How could she be so wrong? Should she have kept fighting for Cash? What was she being punished for now? She just wanted someone to tell her things were going to be all right so she called her house to confront Chuck about what was going on. It took him a while to answer and when he did she could tell that someone else besides him was there. He said it was the next-door neighbor and it quite possibly was but there was more going on that he was trying to make her believe so she hung up the phone.

Leah wanted to call Cash so badly but she didn't. The last time she'd seen him he made it perfectly clear that he didn't think Chuck could take care of them and she didn't feel like hearing "I told you so," so she didn't call him. Of course it would be just a matter of hours before everyone in Page Manor knew that she'd left Chuck and was back living with Gary and Anna including Cash. When the phone rang the next morning she expected it to be Cash but it was Chuck with another attempt to lie his way through. He had a way of mixing the truth with a lie and this morning was no different.

He told Leah that the lights were back on, which she knew was true because Gary took him to pay it. He also stuck to his guns about the neighbors being at their house the night before, sort of true except it was the neighbor's sister there to comfort him, and he said he had a meeting with the recruiter and that he'd finally lost the weight necessary to go to boot camp. Leah just didn't trust him and with good reason. She congratulated him and told him she wasn't coming back until she'd thought some things through.

Chuck told her again the reason he didn't want to tell her about his problems was because he didn't want to worry her but this time he added that he felt her family and friends would judge him. He asked if she'd told Cash about their situation and when she said she hadn't he said, "Now who's lying?" She told him she hadn't but he would be her next call and hung up. She had no intentions of calling Cash or anyone else. She really wanted to figure this thing out. What was the truth and what was a lie. They had been through a lot together; all of it couldn't be a lie, could it? As it turned out he did have a meeting with his recruiter and had lost the necessary weight to go into boot camp but they had so many other unsolved issues. Leah kept her sisters van one day so that she could go to the house and get some things from there before the bailiff came to put them out. She was collecting things when she looked under the bed for a shoe and saw a piece of clothing. She pulled it out and much to her surprise it was a pair of underwear that did not belong to her. As far as she was concerned this was over. She had been keeping to herself, not talking to anyone. Especially not Cash who'd been sending her all sorts of messages through different people including Gary who had asked him not to call the house. She felt so stupid. Not anymore, she would do what she wanted with whomever she wanted and Cash would be first on the list.

That night she told her sister and brother-in-law what she'd found at the house and they agreed that it was time for her to cut him loose until he got himself together. Gary laughed and said he knew at least one person that would be happy to hear about the breakup. As Chuck prepared for his future in the army, Leah went through the motions with school and family. It wouldn't be long before she would reach out to Cash, and when she did he would be there to give her what she thought she wanted only for Leah to find out, it was not enough.

Chuck left for the army and Leah would be with Cash a few times after that but he was still in the same predicament he was before. The relationship they'd shared had changed and even the intimacy they once shared wasn't enough. Chuck began to pay back the money he owed and make preparations for Leah and Bianca to join him. When it was evident that Leah was leaving Cash made one last attempt at changing her mind.

He took her to Cincinnati for the weekend, where he wined and dined her using every opportunity he found to tell her that Chuck could not be trusted. Leah knew he was probably right but she knew for certain that there was no future for her with Cash and she told him that. Still, they spent the weekend making love and ended it by going to a football game where the Steelers, (Cash's home team) got beat badly by the Bengals. They laughed all the way home promising to stay friends and keep in touch. Leah wished things had turned out different. She still wanted to be Cash's wife but because of the kind of man he was he wouldn't leave his family. That was one of the reasons she loved him.

Leah went back to Detroit to prepare for she and Bianca to go to Virginia where they'd stationed Chuck. Chuck was coming home on his first leave and they were going to be married. Everything was in order and in place. Leah ignored the times that she'd called for Chuck and he wasn't available. She just kept planning for her wedding. Chuck was coming home in a month and they were getting married. Leah started to feel really tired all of the time and the first morning that she got sick she knew exactly what the problem was. She was pregnant!

Adding to the problem was the fact that she didn't know who the father was. She didn't tell Cash, or anybody at first. Chuck was in South Carolina finishing his training before going to Virginia. The news of her pregnancy threw him for a loop because she made no secret of the fact that she'd been with Cash. Leah was honest with him, she told she didn't know for sure which of them was the father, but she believed and wanted it to be him. That was good enough for Chuck, whatever/whoever else he was doing he wanted Leah as his wife and if he had to raise another mans baby to make that happen he would, he was already doing that for Bianca. Not to mention he felt a little responsible for Leah ending up going back to Cash.

Chuck came home in the midst of a horrible storm. The two of them rented a car and drove in the middle of that storm to Toledo and got married. Driving home the storm was so bad they had to pull over on the side of the road. Leah began to cry, she was so afraid of what the future held. The winds pushed the car from one side of the road to another. They didn't have money for a room so they had to keep driving. On the way home Leah began to wonder what her life would be like from now on. What if this was Cash's baby? It didn't matter she was married now. She had lots of what if questions for herself but the answer was the same, "It didn't matter, she was married now."

Leah got married for all of the wrong reasons but she was married. Years of infidelity and lack of responsibility would take its toll on their marriage. Circumstances would continue to push Leah toward the only comfort that she could find, in drugs and alcohol. In the sequels to come Leah desperately looks for the love she is sure that she can find in men only to discover that concept of love is a fleeing fantasy for her. In her desperation she loses everything, husband, children and even herself to a world that she never should have been a part of. But God!! Join her as she continues her journey, On The Way Here!

To my sisters that are currently struggling with issues of incest, abusive relationships, or addictions of any kind, know that you are loved and that you are not alone. Find A Place Of Safety!!!! A new beginning awaits you!! There are local women's shelters in every town, contact them now!!! From there you can choose your new path!!! I chose God and I don't regret it!!!!

CPSIA information can be obtained at www.ICGtesting.com
Printed in the USA
BVOW072322190112

280964BV00002B/35/P